SUPER-CHARGED

RETIREMENT

DITCH the ROCKING CHAIR,
TRASH the REMOTE,
and DO WHAT YOU LOVE

MARY LLOYD

Hankfritz Press

Published by Hankfritz Press
Hankfritz Press
4615 29th Ave. NE
Tacoma, WA 98422

Cover design by Greenleaf Book Group LLC
Interior design and composition by Kathryn E. Campbell

ISBN 13: 978-0-9798319-8-0

Library of Congress Control Number: 2008907834

Printed in the United States of America on acid-free paper

First Edition

To all those who made this book possible,

either with your kind and generous support

or by making me frustrated enough

to start beating this drum

Contents

ACKNOWLEDGMENTS

THANK YOU. Thank you. Thank you.

So many did so much to make this happen. I wanted to be sure to give you each a special nod and even started a list early in the process. Then I realized it's not nice to implicate friends and family in a revolution by reference. So I will keep it general here. You know who you are—many of you know who each other are. Thank you all so much to the following:

Those I spoke with in various conversations who knew exactly what I was talking about when I said "invisible" and "irrelevant." You made me realize I needed to do something about it.

Those who served as the initial deadline providers, even when you didn't have time to read the chapters. It would not have happened without you.

Those who gave me feedback, chapter by chapter. You kept me on the right road.

Those who read the full draft of the manuscript and told me what needed to be tweaked and to keep going. You made it so much better.

My critique group, for advice and encouragement way beyond writing. You kept me going.

Those who've provided business advice. You helped me see so far beyond "needing to write a book."

My family—siblings, kids, and kids-in-law. You are all awesome. I sure lucked out in the familial lottery.

Those who helped me relax in the middle of all of it, especially recently. You made it so much easier.

Thank you to all of you for your support, candor, input, assistance, love, and respect. You have my deepest gratitude and love.

Mary Lloyd
January 30, 2009

SUPER-CHARGED

RETIREMENT

DITCH THE ROCKING CHAIR, TRASH THE REMOTE, AND DO WHAT YOU LOVE

Introduction:

A Few Preliminary Remarks

WHEN YOU CAN AFFORD NOT TO WORK ALL DAY every day, the real prize is not the leisure. It's the chance to begin again in a direction that reflects who you've become. It took me an excruciatingly long time to figure that out—which is why my path includes writing this book. If I can help even one person get to the good stuff faster, I will be pleased.

Once we retire, the vast majority of us become virtually invisible. We're stereotyped as out of shape, in need of huge amounts of medical attention, and focused on grandchildren and finding the right retirement community. The expectation of our culture is that it's only a matter of time until we will be a burden to our children and to society in general. Those paying into Social Security with dollars they would rather have for themselves believe we already are.

This is hogwash, of course, but commonly held hogwash. We need to shed light on the real options for people who have reached the point where they no longer have to work. We need to see the truth—that when you leave, you may have as much of your life left to live as you spent in the workforce. People are living to 100. Acting like everything is over when you turn 62 is ridiculous. But society assumes we are "done" once presented with the gold watch and the gag gifts.

There's so much life left in us when we reach this point. There's so much to gain by claiming it. If we live our lives authentically after we "retire," we will be healthier physically, emotionally, spiritually. But, more importantly, we will be on fire with life. That fire can light the way, warm hearts, and get a lot of good stuff cooking.

We need to change the way we undertake this transition. Our assumptions and expectations of the years after we retire need to change—individually and as a society. Those of us who have gotten that far, need to stand up and say confidently, "No, that's not me at all." And then go out and be who we really are.

This book is designed to help light that new path. It's here to help you affirm who you are now—who you've become over all these years—so you can make retirement decisions that keep you vibrant and energized. It's here to debunk the myths about what's "possible" and to lay the groundwork for your own best life.

The chapters are fairly self-explanatory. In the first three, we go from exploring the general idea, to the tools that will serve you best, and then on to a preliminary run at gathering information about who you are and what's important to you. From there we go into four specialized sections—physical considerations and then, in succeeding chapters, mental, emotional, and spiritual aspects. The grand finale is a comprehensive assessment chapter to help you try to weave it all together. Don't panic if you aren't ready for that chapter—or if you decide to do it again and again or "later." The purpose of the book is to help you figure out where you are and where you want to go next. We aren't all going the same place and we aren't traveling at the same speed. Be yourself—but stay accountable. No one is going to do this for you. I guarantee it.

Each chapter also has a predictable structure. They start with a discussion of the topic that draws on diverse sources—sort of a travelogue of the territory you'll be in for that chapter. The studies and quotes mentioned are elaborated on in the Chapter Notes at the end of the book. The second part provides a series of exercises aimed at helping you gather information about yourself on that topic. You'll get a lot more out of this if you do them. Really.

The last section is anecdotal. Consider it your reward for putting all that work into the assessment stuff. This part is my story—or the part of it that relates to the topic at hand. Sometimes it's nice to know someone else has screwed it up worse than you ever could. I've pretty much done that on all fronts with this transition. Feel free to learn from my mistakes.

My sincerest wish is that the book wakes you to the excitement of this stage of life. We are not done. Many of us are barely started. Our time after retirement is full of potential. Our talents and our energy are still there to use. There is no law keeping us on the bench—or in the rocking chair. We are the ones making the choices. We need to find what we believe in and do it. There's a lot of fun yet to be had. A lot of good yet to be done. Your personal piece of that is waiting for you to figure it out. Welcome to the grandest of all life's adventures.

CHAPTER ONE:

OUT THE DOOR AND
OVER THE CLIFF

THE FIRST TIME I SAW THE GRAND CANYON, one of the things that intrigued me was whether anyone had ever gone over the edge before they realized it was there. You can't see it until you are on top of it if you are coming out of the pine forest. On horseback and going fast, a cowboy or desperado might have found himself in free fall before he knew what was happening.

Retirement is a lot like that. For the most part, we come roaring up to it at top career speed and pitch headlong into a world much different than the one we were in three seconds ago without realizing the magnitude of the change.

It's not just about having enough money. We plan weeklong vacations with more diligence than the two, three, or even four decades we will live after we leave the workforce. This is understandable. Our communal vision of "retirement" is being able to do what we want when we want and nothing else. Planning implies structure and structure is the last thing we want when we walk out that workplace door for the last time.

The end of mindless meetings, stuck-in-traffic commuting, irritating interference from the office nemesis, and other such negatives is the primary focus. No more neckties—or pantyhose. No more monthly progress notes or grading papers. No more having to accept someone else's right to decide how you're going to spend huge chunks of your time. And, of course, no more stress. Just hour after lovely hour of doing whatever you want.

Or so the fantasy goes. It's the antithesis of planning.

The idea that you work until you are 62 or 67 (or whenever your birth year establishes you as "eligible" with the Social Security Administration) and then just stop and go off and play is our current Big Lie as a society. It's not what's happening or, more importantly, what needs to happen for everyone's good. True, some are voluntarily working longer before ever taking retirement. But nearly a quarter of the workers who say they are "retired" still work either full or part time. According to a study done by Merrill Lynch's retirement group, two thirds of Americans claim they will do some kind of work for pay in retirement.

At the same time, ageism is real and continues to be pervasive, according to Dr. Robert Butler, of the Longevity Center in New York, who's been studying it since 1968. Determining the work you want to do for pay after retirement and finding it will involve an entirely different strategy and process than we used out of high school or even in the downturns of the last few decades. But work we must. Work is about more than money and we need it in some form to thrive. As a nation, we are just now starting to realize this.

DO I HAVE TO?

More and more, those starting to think about retirement are asking if it's even what they really want. Usually, there's something that makes continuing in the current work situation unappealing. Office politics. The commute. A desire to live somewhere else. But there are also things about the life of ease suggested as "retirement" that are worrisome. Just how good can you get at "doing nothing?" And how good do you want to be?

Is the next step simply not working? Or do you want to redesign your life so it contains everything you want in the proportions you prefer personally? Are you looking for a rocking chair or a launching pad? A nap or an adventure?

In a recent article, Rosabeth Moss Kanter—Harvard management professor and corporate guru—noted that those now on the brink of retiring are not likely to make this transition quietly as a group. "Having been told from birth about their own significance [thanks in a large part to the advice of Dr. Benjamin Spock], they aren't going to feel less significant simply because they've hit a career ceiling called retirement age." She cites research done by Met Life and Civic Ventures where the majority of the Americans between 50 and 70 who were asked said they wanted to benefit their communities in some way with what they do with their time and/or for a living at this point in their lives. This is only one of the differences between our venerated image of "the golden years" and the reality of what they will be like once the baby boom steps into them.

"Retirement" is the wrong word altogether. "Retire" per good old Webster's is "to withdraw from action or danger: RETREAT; to move back: RECEDE; to withdraw from circulation or the market: RECALL." Why would anybody want to do that at the top of their game?" Why would anyone want to do that *ever* unless they were sick, tired, or both?

Good question. But this is a new paradigm, and the answer is still in the works. For the time being, those of us asking are going to have to figure it out for ourselves. And since, by this point in our lives, we are all incredibly unique, the answers aren't going to be the same for all of us. That will be true even when the resources and roadmaps needed to do this smoothly are in place—which they aren't yet.

These answers are probably not going to be easy to figure out for you specifically either. Why should they be? You might be looking at as much as 40 or 50 percent of your total life span in what remains. What do you want to do with all that? What is important to get done? And how do you want to go about it? How do you LIKE to do things?

These are the more important questions about retirement. The point at which you are well enough off to give up a regular job and rely on the sources of income you've secured that don't require your hours and days is not really "retirement." It's just another graduation—like high school and college. Congratulations! You have met all the requirements to be allowed to move on to the next level of life. Like all graduations, this involves a *commencement*. A beginning.

We are not looking at "old age" when we turn 60. If Hugh Hefner is right, "80 is the new 40." (And yes, he is still living like he's 40 and the king of *Playboy*, from the sound of it.) In her book, *Don't Stop the Career Clock*, Helen Harkness suggests that the point at which we are usually looking at retirement options is actually "the second midlife." "Retiring" provides the chance to exit the current work situation gracefully—usually with at least a partial financial safety net—and begin again, reconnecting with "calling" as the compass for charting a new course. She refers to this transition to more meaningful work as "the capstone career."

I believe it goes farther than that. For many of us, this phase of our lives will involve more than one "career" and more than one direction, perhaps even simultaneously. These are the best years, characterized by action, direction, and passion. And a big dose of flexibility. It is the time of our lives where what we do next can make a profound positive difference if we so choose and we have the energy, stamina, and focus to make that happen. It is also the time of our lives where we owe it to society to model balance in how we go about it. The years are the best because we do good things for others, but they are also the best because we have designed a quality lifestyle for ourselves. We do what we want, but that includes doing good.

For many, that "good" is likely to be on a paid basis. People who get paid to do things tend to have more clout and more credibility than those acting as volunteers. "Work" also provides a better framework for focus and goal setting. But it won't look like the work we are leaving.

We will not do 60-hour workweeks on a regular basis, but we may push that hard for a few days to get a specific project through a critical phase. Then we'll take a month off to hike at Mount Rainier or sail the Sea of Cortez or help a niece who lives 2000 miles away deal with newborn twins.

We'll focus our experience and well-honed management and leadership talents on whatever project we've agreed to get done. But we will also explore the wonders of Egypt or take a class in making art glass. This is the time to create beautiful lives. Meaningful lives in terms of our own uniqueness. Lives that give those still trudging along in standard career mode inspiration to keep going. It is not about giving up work. It's about working at what we want, at what we think is important and therefore worth doing. It is also about shaping the work we choose so it doesn't exclude the other things we want in our lives.

Not every one will want this choice. Some people really are tired and don't want to have to worry about anything—at least for a while. Some people will retire and won't decide they need more meaning in their lives until several years or even decades after they leave the workforce. The beauty of this new dawn is that it's not a "one size must fit all" situation. It's not even a "one size fits the same person forever" situation. If you have the money to lie on the beach year round and that's what you want to do, it's your call. Nobody is going to tell you to go back to work. If you want to lie on the beach this year and get involved in making an inner city youth program financially stable next year, it's still your call.

Take heart if you have the chance to retire and are hesitating. There is so much left. So much to explore. So much to learn. So much to become part of and make happen. The stereotype suggests there is nothing out there but cruise tours and golf. But it's really a matter of personal choice. The key is figuring out what the best version of this time in your life looks like for you. What excites you? What brings you satisfaction? How do you like to learn things? What do you want to learn? It's time to roll up your sleeves. As Dr. Seuess advises, "You're off to Great Places. Today is your day! Your mountain is waiting. So…*get on your way!*"

There is, however, a caveat. The model is still under construction. Many of the resources we need to figure it out don't exist. Yet. Many of the tasks that we could do well and to society's benefit haven't been defined. Yet. The landmarks are still in the mist. We will have to explore them individually and up close for a while before they become part of a readily available map. Even this is fitting. The folks preparing to start this adventure are the "leading edge boomers"—those who grew up in the 1960s. The folks who brought you—for better and/or worse—Vietnam War protests, civil rights marches, and free love. A group Kanter describes as naturally feeling like world changers. Only this time around, they are teetering on the brink of wisdom. "Me" is less of an issue now. "Us" is in.

Do I Have Enough Credits?

HARD FACTS DEAL BREAKERS

"Giving up work," as a British friend describes it, is a uniquely personal decision. It is also a uniquely complex one. The ramifications affect every single area of your life—from the obvious ones like finances to the less apparent ones like health and relationships.

A recent article in *US News & World Report* noted that in terms of cold cash, working longer is a financial hat trick. You have more years in which to save for retirement. You have fewer years where you will have to live off your savings. And you will be able to draw a larger payment from Social Security once you enroll. As a bonus, you can also keep your healthcare coverage longer. But at some point, it's time to stop.

Sometimes, this moment is defined by external forces. Per AARP, 40 percent of us will retire unexpectedly, either because of health problems or company changes. You might be caught in a downsizing or a "realignment of business." You might be in the perfect position to sell the business you've built at a handsome price if you act immediately. You might be forced to retire because you've reached a mandatory age, as airline pilots are. External forces make the initial decision easier—often it's not even yours. But the work to get it right once you go over the cliff is the same.

But what if this *is* your decision? No one is pushing you with a RIF or a buy-out or a management shake-up. You're just starting to feel "It's time for something else." How do you decide if you are ready and if you really want to?

The first issue, is, of course, the economics. Do you have enough money? There are enough books, seminars, and consultants to work through this question 12 times over. So we will not dwell on it here. But it is the initial deal breaker. You have to have enough to live on. If you are mortgaged to the hilt, have credit card debt that will take years to pay off even at your current income level, and no plan for a "retirement" career in place, you need to keep doing what you're doing. Or else find other, more satisfying work you can continue to do on a fulltime basis.

If you do have enough money, the question becomes do you WANT to retire?

The first branch on this part of the decision tree is do you like what you are doing? Does it still excite you? Is it an area that you could work in until the very last day of your life and feel good that it was how you spent all your time? If the answer is no and you know you can retire if you want to, maybe it's time to graduate to something that's more fun, more interesting, and leaves you more on fire at the end of the day.

If the answer is yes, then on to the next question. Is the outfit you are currently working for the place to do this work? Is it supportive? Do they appreciate what you can do and give you the chance to do it well? Do you feel like you are working to your full potential in the assignments you're given? If the answer is no, then it may still be time to retire, but to reinvent yourself in the same field in a way that gives you more room to grow.

The next question considers the context you're working in. Are the company you're working for and the work you are doing for it stable? Is this job going to be around indefinitely? For example, the options markets are moving toward electronic trading. If you make your living in open outcry activities in a trading pit, don't bank on having the same job for another 15 years.

If you love what you do and who you do it for and the situation is not going to change anytime soon, you don't need retirement, you need to play the lottery. The vast majority of us are not that lucky.

There are other initial deal breakers. For example, legal considerations. You could be under a contract that requires you to finish out or face a stiff penalty. There could be family issues. Do you need the health insurance not to change right now because of a family member's situation? My lacrosse-playing son required knee surgery when I was making my decision. As long as I stayed with the company, he was fully covered for the procedure. Delaying my departure until he could have the knee repaired made perfect sense.

"TOUCHY FEELY" FACTORS

Factual considerations tend to focus on why NOT to retire. Can't afford it. Can't get the company scholarship for my daughter if I do, etc. The next set of questions deals with why you DO want to retire. They are lifestyle questions. The work pace and stress level in our employment culture can be obscene or downright lethal. If the only thing you are doing is your job because that's all you have the time and energy for, it's time to leave if it's feasible for you to retire. (Unless, of course, you love your work so much that it's all you *want* to do.)

Does what you are doing now give you room to do all the other things that are important to you? Are the hours reasonable enough to let you maintain your physical health, family ties, and personal social contacts? Do you travel about as much as you'd like for the job and for fun? If not, this is the time of life where you can create your own version of a job/life mix.

Where are you getting your emotional support? Where are you getting your sense of community and belonging? Where are you getting your creative satisfaction? What level of activity do you need to feel satisfied? How much "new" do you need in your life?

This is where things can melt down quickly. Most of us have functioned in the realm of facts and quantifiable aspects in what we do for a living. The idea of being able to describe what you like, want, and need seems counterintuitive. If I like it, I don't need to even think about it—it's just there. Not exactly.

In the movie *The Runaway Bride* Richard Gere accuses Julia Roberts of knowing so little about herself that she can't even tell him how she likes her eggs cooked for breakfast. In a later scene, she tastes eggs, cooked all different ways, and actually decides. She'd been liking her eggs the way whoever she was with liked them for her entire adult life. We all do that—perhaps not with breakfast, but with a whole lot of more essential stuff. I played golf—or tried hard to learn—for 10 years. I abhor activities with lots of rules. What was I thinking? I have lived and floated around on cruise ships 96 days of my life. It took me until the 93rd of those days to accept that I get seasick on cruises and the version I get lasts about a month, whether I remain on a ship or not.

This is not just a "girl" thing. We do things to accommodate the people we care about. We make choices in that context and then forget it was the context that defined the choice. We need to look at things again without that context defining them.

To get an accurate idea of what you like and to establish the specs of the blueprint for your best lifestyle, you have to do the research. Assuming you already know—when you haven't done a second of reflection about it—is likely to leave you staring numbly into empty space at some point when the novelty of doing whatever you want whenever you want wears off. Take the time to check it out before you set off. Trying to figure it out later is a lot harder. Trust me on this. It is not fun wandering around in the fog in the dark, year after year. Figure out what you like, what you want in your life, and how you want to go about getting it. THEN go after it. Assuming that it will just show up as soon as you quit work is way beyond dumb, even if it is the default strategy we are all currently offered.

Think and Do

My absolute favorite part of school when I was a kid was a workbook called "Think and Do." It was a companion book to the reader, where you got to use what you read. First you had to understand the story. Then you had to figure something out with the information that you'd been given. I will forever be a fan of Think and Do. There was always an adventure in those assignments. I hope the Think and Do sections of this book generate that same sense of adventure for you.

Important decisions warrant effective decision-making and what you want to do with the rest of your life is a very important decision. The legitimacy of information used is one of the keys to good decisions. We are bombarded with information and persuasion dressed as "advice" day and night. However, the decisions to be made about retirement are best made from information you'll never see on television or find on the Internet. It needs to come from within you. This seems like it should be easy, but it's not. The volume of external information we are subjected to buries the internal information and makes it hard to access with certainty.

You may have already answered all the questions about whether or not you are in a position to retire with total accuracy. In fact, you may have already jumped off that cliff and are now starting to look at whether it's what you want to keep doing. Either way, it's good to double check to be sure you are working with accurate information. It's way too easy to use thinking that came from other people or the media and believe it's really your own. Your decisions about what you want to do with you life need to be based on who you are when there is no one and nothing influencing you.

To get you started, this chapter offers some career-specific "Think and Do." These exercises go beyond the yes/no answers of the decision tree we just went through and explore your own reality more thoroughly. The job of Think and Do, as we'll use it here, is to gather information from inside you and organize it in a way that helps make your path to important decisions more straightforward. The more sincere and open you are in doing the exercises, the more relevant, accurate and useful the information will be. That said, doing them with your sense of humor turned on is also important. There's more than salad dressing and beer that's best done "lite" if we want to live healthy.

Yes, yes, I know. You hate that touchy feely, introspective stuff. You don't want to dwell on how awful it was to be the last kid chosen for the kickball game in third grade or having to visit your great grandmother in the nursing home when you were sixteen. I don't either. Which is good, because that's not where this is going at all. But you're going to need information to get this project going right and you're the one who has it. Think and Do is an easy way to pull it out and look at it.

In all the chapters, the Think and Do exercises are about NOW. About your current priorities and values. About what you like, don't like, and might like because of who you've grown to be. I promise I will not ask you to do a timeline of your life, draw pictures of your pet with your non-dominant hand, or write a list of all the people you need to forgive or ask forgiveness of. You can do all that stuff if you want, but it's not what we need for this. What's essential for these decisions is to learn as much as you can about you as you exist here and now.

Chapter One's Think and Do involves two different ways to look at your work situation. Also, since some readers are likely to have already left the workforce, there are two versions of these two exercises. "Before the Door" is for those who are still employed but thinking about retirement. "After the Cliff" is for those already retired who want to explore new options. In both, the best answers are the first ones—before you start to think and say what would sound good, look good, or be the best thing to have said if your spouse—or boss—ever found your answers.

If you want complete security, rip the pages out and shred them once you've learned what you need to know. On the other hand, if you want to talk about it with your brother, mother, spouse, eldest son, or the next person in line at the grocery store once you discover these personal touchstones, that works, too.

And do them as fun. This is an exploration of terrain that should be especially interesting to you. Go at it like a kid on a neighborhood adventure. Think and Do runs on two levels here. I want you to think and do the exercises, sure. But that's only so that you can think and do what's needed for you to live a life that has you smiling most of the time.

VERSION A: Before the Door
For those still in the workforce.

Exercise 1.1A—THIS JOB AND THIS COMPANY

Rate each of the following statements in terms of how accurate it is for you on this job at this point in time. Put a number between 1 and 9 in the open box of each statement.

RATING VALUES

Not at all like me: 1 2 3 4 5 6 7 8 9 : Totally me

What I do in my job is important.			
Other people think I have the perfect job.			
I like the flexibility the company gives me.			
I need more time for myself to stay healthy.			
Even after a hard day, I'm excited about my work.			
My spouse is very proud of me for having this job.			
I'm proud of the company I work for.			
There is a lot of negative stress on this job.			
This job gives me fun challenges to meet.			
Most of my friends are coworkers.			
My company appreciates me.			
I need to know more than I do about what's going on at work.			
The work I do on this job is interesting.			
The people I work with are the most important part of this job.			
This company is financially sound.			
Management here doesn't care what workers think.			

What I do on my job is good for people and society.				
This job has high prestige and I like that.				
I enjoy the teamwork and work environment at this company.				
I feel like a fraud and a cheat to be doing this work.				
TOTALS: Total the numbers in each column. The highest possible score for a column is 45. The lowest is 5.				

The first column deals with your satisfaction level with the kind of work you do. If this score is high, you are doing work that has meaning for you. If you want to "retire," graduating to an arrangement that gives you the chance to continue doing this kind of work but with enhanced lifestyle elements you value (e.g. fewer hours, work schedule flexibility, more vacation time, etc.) might be a good strategy.

The second column deals with social factors. If this score is high, it means you are likely to be affected by the loss of social contacts and the prestige you or your family/friends value in the position you now hold. Finding other ways to fill this need will be an important part of your transition if you choose to retire.

The third column looks at how you feel about the company you work for. If column one is high and column three is low, you may not want to retire at all, but rather change companies. If column three is high and column one is low, going in a new direction within the company might be worth looking at, particularly if you can negotiate enhanced lifestyle elements. If you leave the company, you will be losing that strong sense of belonging. You may need to find other sources to satisfy this need.

The fourth column is a quick read on overall job dissatisfaction. This is different than simply being low on satisfaction scores. Dissatisfaction factors are typically sources of negative stress, which can cause illness. If this score is high, leaving is likely to feel like emancipation.

Exercise 1.2A—SHOOTING FROM THE HIP

*Answer these with the first thing that comes
into your mind (including smart remarks and jokes).*

The thing I like most about the job I'm doing now is _____

_____

_____

If I did this for a different employer _____

_____

_____

The thing I dislike about what I am doing now is _____

_____

_____

If I knew I could take six months to do whatever I want and then come
back to this job _____

_____

_____

If I could take a year off and had this job to come back to _____

_____

_____

If I did take six months or a year, my feelings about the job would _____

_____

_____

If I knew that whatever I tried was going to turn out exactly as I need a
want it to _____

_____

_____

If I knew my family and important friends would approve of anything I decided to do _____

_____

_____

I could do this job until the day I die if _____

_____

_____

When I think about leaving this job _____

_____

_____

Sentence completion exercises often yield unexpected information. Go back and look at your replies. If any of them surprise you enough to dig deeper, try the following:

The answer about _____ surprises me because _____

_____

_____

My answer about _____ excites me because _____

_____

_____

If your initial reply was a joke or a smart remark and you want to dig deeper, you can try

When I said that, it was a way to _____

_____

_____

I am surprised I can make a joke about that because _____

_____

_____

VERSION B: AFTER THE CLIFF
For those who have already left the workforce.

Exercise 1.1B—THE REALITY OF FREE FALL

Rate each of the following statements in terms of how accurate it is for you at this point in time. Put a number between 1 and 9 in the open box of each statement.

RATING VALUES

Not at all like me: 1 2 3 4 5 6 7 8 9 **: Totally me**

I am totally comfortable with how I use my time.				
Not having money coming in bothers me.				
I feel isolated now that I don't have work as a way to connect.				
I could help many ways but no one will let me do what I can.				
I love being able to putter all day long.				
I worry that I am going to run out of money.				
I don't have people that I consider good friends to do things with.				
I feel invisible.				
I like not having to make plans for what I do each day.				
I am not willing to spend money for things I used to buy readily.				
I feel isolated.				
It bothers me that I am not contributing in some way.				
My retirement could not be better.				
I worry about the stock market and/or the security of my pension.				
No one wants all the skills and experience I am ready to offer.				

There's got to be more than this.			
I would not change a thing about my life in retirement.			
I need more cash coming in than I have now.			
I want to be more involved with other people.			
I need something to make me want to get out of bed every day.			
TOTALS: Total the numbers in each column. The highest possible score for a column is 45. The lowest is 5.			

The first column deals with your satisfaction level with retirement in general. If this score is high, the lifestyle you are living works. At most, you are likely to want to tweak it a bit, but major changes may not be necessary. Then again, you may be deluding yourself about how much you like retirement. Go for a walk by yourself and think about it if you aren't sure.

The second column deals with how you feel about your current financial situation. Though your financial situation may have deteriorated for some reason, concerns of this type are often not a reflection of the actual state of your finances. For many people, spending the money that's been saved—even if that is exactly what it was saved for—is very difficult. If this number is high, finding a way to create even a small cash flow from active income might be appealing

The third column deals with social factors. If this score is high, it means you need more social contact than your current lifestyle includes. Work is only one way of filling this set of needs and your personality has a lot to do with what is likely to work best. For example, if you prefer to "talk shop" as a way to interact with people, work is probably a better fit than joining a social club. But if you like to dance or play cards to share time with others, then the reverse is more likely to be true.

The fourth column is about how much meaning you find in your life. If this number is high, you may be feeling hollow or restless. The only way to solve this one for good is to uncover your purpose—the thing that you want to do with your life that leaves you feeling excited no matter how tired you are after working at it for the day. Purpose and passion go hand in hand. If you know what you are here to do, it's a lot easier to "get out of bed in the morning."

Exercise 1.2B.—SHOOTING IN MIDAIR

Answer these with the first thing that comes into your mind (including smart remarks and jokes).

The thing I like most about being retired is _____

_____

_____

The thing I didn't expect about retirement is _____

_____

_____

The money thing _____

_____

_____

If I had known retirement was going to be like this _____

_____

_____

My choices about how I spend my time _____

_____

_____

My volunteer experience _____

_____

_____

_____

If I had to do it again, I would _____

_____

_____

My life would be perfect if _____

_____

_____

My life would be almost perfect if _____

_____

_____

For me, the word "retirement" means _____

_____

_____

Sentence completion exercises often yield unexpected information.
Go back and look at your replies. If any of them surprise you
enough to dig deeper, try the following:

The answer about _____ surprises me because _____

_____

My answer about _____ excites me because _____

_____

If your initial reply was a joke or a smart remark
and you want to dig deeper, you can try

When I said that, it was a way to _____

_____

_____

I am surprised I can make a joke about that because _____

_____

_____

How NOT to Do It

My qualifications for writing this book rest heavily on the monumental mess I've made of this process myself. I left work way too early (age 47) for noble reasons and with little planning. I have been at this for 13 years now. I am a virtuoso at what NOT to do. I have gone down every blind alley but alcohol and drugs and have barked up more wrong trees than a near-sighted coon dog.

When I left corporate America, I was intent on pursuing "my last career." Ever since high school, I've expected to be a writer eventually. But there were a few details it would have been good to have taken the time to define at the outset. For starters, my "careers" usually last seven years maximum. I started as a geologist with stops as a stay-at-home mom, a college instructor, a line manager in the utility business, a marketing consultant, an outplacement specialist, several versions of contract specialist, and several levels as an executive manager in the natural gas industry before I got to "writer." The job I was leaving was as head of gas supply for a major combination utility. It had taken me about 25 years to do all that. What made me think writing was going to hold my attention for 30 or 40 or even 50 years all by itself?

I *am* a writer. That was true then and is true now. But I am also a lot of things that don't get honored if I focus only on writing. My first big mistake was assuming I could, should, and would be a one-channel person. Never have been. Never gonna be. I need a lot of different things going on for life to be good. You do not want to know how long it took me to admit that.

I also did an abysmal job of making an accurate inventory of where my support resided. My spouse was in favor of my leaving the corporate rat race. He encouraged me to "play the song." (The song was "Take This Job and Shove It.") But many of the things that confirmed my value for me internally were in the work setting. There, I was perceived as competent and a resource to others. There, I got to solve complex problems as part of a team of intelligent, fun, enthusiastic peers. There, I knew how to do what needed to be done and got regular feedback—from customers and performance measures—that I was doing it well. When I chose leaving as a way to take a stand on something that definitely needed to be addressed, I left all that behind. Without it, there wasn't much to remind me of all the things I could do well.

I'm a good cook and, at that point, I was decent at keeping house and doing the June Cleaver things. But those were not (and are not) *important* skills for me. Having someone tell me I make great chocolate chip cookies doesn't have the same impact on my self worth as having someone tell me I've done a great presentation to the board of directors. I came across as competent to my spouse, sons, stepdaughters, and neighbors, but before very long I totally lost my sense of competence in terms of what I thought of myself.

I did jump headlong into learning to write, so there were challenges. There is a lot more to good fiction than writing about something that happened to you that was "interesting." There is a lot more to selling *any* kind of writing than I ever imagined.

I naively believed I would be a published novelist in a year—two at most. I'm *still* trying to make that happen.

The trouble was not with whether I'm capable of good writing. From the beginning, I've gotten good feedback about my potential. Even an impossible workshop leader—a curmudgeon who annihilated the writing sample I'd submitted for his review in front of 50 of my peers—told me I knew *how* to write. He also advised me I did not know *what* to write. Dammit. He was spot on.

Thing after thing got in the way of me letting myself become a published author. I would write regularly for a few weeks or months until some family project took me away for a month or two. Then I'd need a month or two to re-establish my focus and tone so I could get on with the writing project. I did a lot of "60-page abortions," too. Those were the ideas that fizzled after three weeks or a month of working on them. Often, I would just give up on them after I'd gotten distracted by the rest of my life, but sometimes I put them away because "no one would want to read this. I'm not credible enough…or funny enough…or interesting enough."

When I completed my first novel, I let it rest as the gurus advised, and then revised it with the help of a fantastic critique group. I finally began trying to sell it nearly THREE years after I'd left work "to become a writer." By then, we had sold the family business, and my husband and I had begun to travel. This was when cell phones were still optional, exotic equipment. My spouse was Welsh by heritage. He lived by the adage "A Welshman can live on what a Scot throws away." No way would a cell phone have been part of our travel gear even if I had suggested it. Which I didn't.

Every time we left town on a trip, I'd worry one of the agents I'd queried might call and want to talk to me while I wasn't there. After a few months, I stopped sending out queries. I wasn't home enough to open the mail much less edit my novel to meet a publisher's requirements.

But one of the great things about being a writer is that everything you do is material. So no matter what else I was doing, I was "working." That idea made my abdication seem totally reasonable. Travel was good for what I was going to "write next." I have been a wanderer since I was old enough to walk. I love to go see "somewhere else". Say the word "trip" and I will immediately pack a bag. And I did get a lot of material. But now, in addition to not knowing *what* to write, I didn't know *when* to write. My sense of competence sank even lower.

We became masters of the fine art of road tripping. The first year after we sold the business, we saw every one of our combined six kids in their own residences, which meant trips to Seattle, Dallas, Chicago, Kansas City, Los Angeles, and Denver. Denver was the only "day trip." We took one full month to explore Florida in January. We went to my niece's wedding in Wisconsin and then on to see Tennessee and the Great Smokey Mountains in the fall. We were traveling fools.

Then came "the Great Adventure." Friends asked if we would be interested in going on a world cruise with them. The word "cruise" got to the guy I was married to. He was ex-Navy. The word "world" got to me. Travel all over the world? Oh yeah.

I kept deluding myself that the not-writing life I was living was just an interlude. That I was really working. That I was not "retired." I just had a job that let me travel all the time and never get anything done.

After the big cruise, travel began to change tone. With road trips, instead of deciding what we wanted to see and the best route to take to do that, we began deciding where we were going based on timeshare availability. I'd agree to organized travel opportunities because they were "a good deal" or because friends wanted to do them—not because it was an adventure I really wanted be on. Trips became something we needed to do to be able to talk about them when we got home. Trips became a way to "get away from the weather" rather than unpredictable adventures to new places (like WaKeeney, Kansas during an April snowstorm). When we got to the destination, the first priority for my spouse was a beer and a dose of CNBC—so it felt just like being at home for him. Once it morphed into this new format, travel was no longer fun for me. But I am a wanderer and was not willing to admit that it was leaving me ever more empty.

We were retired. Yes, we were. Was I retired? No way was I going to admit that. I was a writer. And all that travel was great for stories I was going to write someday.

So we kept on taking trips and doing timeshare weeks and I kept on falling deeper and deeper into a pit I didn't even recognize as such. I suspect the effect was sort of like having your eyesight fail gradually. Finally, it's just too dark to see. Did I see the dark? No. But I did feel the dissonance. I blamed it on living at 6000 feet.

Time for… "The Geography Solution!" The region of the country where we lived was what was making my life so hard. That was what kept me from smiling. Everything would be fine if we lived somewhere else. We needed to move to the Pacific Northwest. That would solve everything.

To be sure, there was a whole lot positive about the move, and I am still glad we did it. But it was not the solution. I spent the next three years feathering a new nest and creating new garden magic—two very enjoyable ways of not being a writer without having to admit I wasn't.

It was fun to start over in making a house a home. It was fun even though we were out in the middle of nowhere and it was a 30-minute trip just to buy a loaf of bread. It was fun because it was different and thus challenging. How could it take me so long to catch on? Challenge—that was what I was really after. Challenge that helped me see myself as capable. Everything I did to keep my life changing was a way to help me feel *competent* as I dealt with the new situations.

In retrospect, the level of complexity I injected into even simple projects was my lifeline. I may not have been writing, but at least I was *thinking*. I was not, however, feeling. Or at least *admitting* what I was feeling. Even with the colossal amount of change I managed to generate, what I was feeling was suffocated, invisible, and dead.

Eventually, it all caught up with me. Things got so black the safest option left was to go on anti-depressants. I hated the idea. But the black void was so overwhelming I knew it was either that or risk doing something stupid and permanent.

I took those lovely little pills for six weeks—just long enough to help me find my gravesite in the emotional cemetery and start digging. I finally admitted two things. What I thought was a good marriage was not. And the person whom everyone else knew and relied on as "me" was not me at all. Oddly, my father's death—a man I adored—after a long, rich life, finally goaded me into action on these two counts. I moved out of the dream home and began to search for myself.

Then I chickened out and moved back in. I decided screenwriting, not novels, was my niche. I took a yearlong online graduate certificate course from UCLA and loved it. What a blast. I do love screenwriting (also writing novels) but I was still trying to do the one-channel thing. I was also trying to do it in a situation that was not at all healthy for me emotionally.

Three years ago, I really did let go of the marriage. I moved to a new city in the same area, closer to family and friends and society in general. I started to join groups doing things I was interested in. I began to make friends of all sorts. I kept up the personal excavation efforts, still totally confused about what it was I was "supposed to be doing."

The dawn finally came when I realized it wasn't just one thing and it would never be just one thing. I need variety and a high level of stimulation in my life. I need complexity. I need fun people who like to do active things. I need to hike. I need to be funny, even zany sometimes. I need to connect with the Divine my own way. It took a major effort just to get to the point of using the words "I need" comfortably.

Am I done? Not even close. But I'm *started*. It would have been a lot easier if I'd gotten a good baseline on who I've grown to be before I left the career cocoon. Thirteen years is a long time wandering around in circles in the dark. It is my most sincere wish that this book helps you avoid the experience.

Chapter Two:

Tools for Excavating Your Life

Q UILTING ALWAYS SEEMED LIKE it would be fun. It's like doing little engineering projects—only with cloth and thread instead of the heavier stuff. But when I started to pursue it as a hobby, I was intimidated by the precise cuts quilting requires. Their necessity is obvious—things are not going to fit together perfectly if they aren't perfectly cut. I assumed all that precision cutting was done with a scissors. If I couldn't use them well enough to cut a clean, long, straight line, I'd never be any good at quilting. Try as I might, I could not cut that clean, long line.

Then someone told me about the rotary cutter.

A rotary cutter is a razor-edged wheel with a handle—also a safety guard and a good grip. It's used with a "self-healing" cutting mat that doesn't disintegrate when cut with the sharp edge of the wheel again and again. Add a big, clear plastic straightedge, lined at quarter-inch intervals and marked with 45 and 60-degree angle lines, and you can cut quilt pieces with the precision of a machine. Lots of them!

The right tools make all the difference. Not only do you have to know how to use them, you have to know they exist. You also have to understand the difference between the entry level tools you've been working with and more sophisticated versions you need for more advanced work.

Using the right tool the right way at the right time. Phew! This tool business is starting to get complicated.

This chapter describes both the tools you must have to make good choices in your life and the tools it's nice to have because they make the process easier. As you go through the collection, be aware of your reactions. That's a tool in itself and quite useful for what we are trying to do here.

To define the best version of a life for these years, you need to make good decisions. To make good decisions, you need to be good at defining the problems you're trying to deal with and generating a broad range of options to consider. So the first set of tools are the problem-solving and decision-making skills—just like in the jobs we've done up to this point. We'll also need persistence and commitment and the ability to communicate effectively—just like up to now. We'll need to set goals and know how to stay on track to meet them. All familiar stuff.

But in addition, there are some new tools. Ever since the scientific method became the standard, intuition has been maligned as a weak substitute for logical thinking. It is, in fact, a separate source and kind of information. For the decisions we need to make now, it has more power than the reasoned logic we've relied on for so long. The ability to access intuitive information will make this work easier.

If you have one of those Y-chromosomes, you may be more comfortable referring to it as "playing your hunches" or "getting a gut feel." But no matter what you call it, being able to get at more than the information offered by your rational mind is important here.

Resistance is actually a tool, as well. The reasons we use for NOT doing what we claim we want to do provide telling insights. Barbara Sher lays this out well in her book, *Live the Life You Love*. She notes "resistance is clear evidence of high self-esteem." (Mine must be in the ozone.) High self-esteem means you plan to survive and survival is usually a case for not doing the scary things. Resistance helps you take the right size steps into your new life. Good tool.

Other abilities that usually aren't considered skills in the logical world will come into play. The ability to hold an idea or a lifestyle in mind without judging it—just to see how it feels; the ability to drift—rather than controlling the direction of your thinking—for a period of time; the ability to surrender control altogether temporarily—so you can see what happens when you do that. All are distinct assets in this research. You don't *have* to be able to do all these things, but it helps.

You *do* have to be able to say "no." Or at least be ready to learn to say it. Saying "no" is an essential tool when you begin any sorting effort. And that's what this is all about. The entire process boils down to what do you like that you want more of in your life and what do you dislike that you want less of? For each thing you examine, you have to be able to say "no" or you aren't sorting at all.

All of these tools run on the same power source—openness. To do any of this work well, you need to be willing to change your mind about the way you've been doing things, seeing things, and prioritizing things. You need to be ready to go in new directions without defining the destination ahead of time. You need to be able to loosen your grip on the familiar long enough that you can eventually let it go. That's the only way your hands will be free to grab onto the new things that are part of the life that's a better fit for you now.

The sorting, the chameleon act of trying on new possibilities, the choices in unexpected directions based on unusual information are all part of growth. Of change. And change is absolutely terrifying. But for every living thing, the options are change or die with every breath. There are a lot of versions of dying and many of them do not involve an actual funeral. Don't do that. I've been there, and it is painful.

The basic question is simple. Do I retire or do I not? The complex question—the one we should make sure we are answering completely and with total honesty—is what do I do once I leave this work?

Solutions and Decisions

When I started to work on this chapter, I got snarled up trying to describe the relationship between problem solving and decision-making. How do they fit together? Is decision making a subset of problem solving or vice versa? What comes first? Decisions are always part of solving a problem, but is a problem required for a decision to be necessary? And what about the second round of problems that come when a decision wasn't made well?

The above was just a nice rational roadblock to keep me from getting on with this. With "The Professor" at the wheel, I can go in circles forever and think I am making progress. Watch for your own version of The Professor. Playing that kind of "thinking game" will keep you from getting to the meat of this for years if you let it. Incidentally, it works fine to lump decision making and problem solving together.

To solve a problem well, you need to:

- Define the problem accurately

- Identify as many solutions as possible

- Evaluate the solutions

- Choose the one that seems to be most effective

- Assess the consequences of that choice and decide again if it's the most effective option.

- Come up with a plan for implementing the decision—an action plan with goals and deadlines.

We do all of our problem solving/decision-making this way, right? If we did, things would be running a lot smoother than they are the world over. Unfortunately, the process often runs more like this:

- Notice what isn't working.

- Do the first thing that comes to mind to make it work.

- Repeat when that solution creates another problem

So what does all this baloney have to do with retirement? A lot. Retirement choices involve problems within problems. We start out looking to solve the two key issues: How do I get more of what I like in my life and less of what I don't like? Then as we identify ways of doing those two things, we end up dealing with a myriad of specific aspects that each involves definition, idea generation, evaluation, selection, and consequence assessment in its own right before we come up with a practical plan—for *that* aspect.

This sounds like an AWFUL lot of work. Luckily, there are other ways to sort that help—but we'll get to that in a minute. For now, let's just look at rationally based decision-making. We do need to do a good job with these decisions. Otherwise we will be making them again and again to solve problem after problem that we've created for ourselves with each previous solution. I have been there. I have done that. Trust me. As a life strategy, it's pathetic.

Take the time to define what you need at its core level—the REAL issue that you need to decide about. Take the time to generate as many solutions as you can. Take the time because it will make life a whole lot easier from here on. More true. More fun. More real.

A few years ago, my husband's daughter asked if we'd be willing to care for their two-year old son for four days so she and her husband could go on a trip he'd won for good performance at work. Of course I said yes. At the same moment I was committing to her, my husband was setting up a timeshare exchange for the two of us in Whistler, British Columbia—for the same week. I'd already agreed to do a timeshare trip. I just didn't know it was going to be that week. In the usual randomness of timeshare availability, we'd ended up with a two-bedroom condo that slept six—for the two of us.

When the kids found out about the situation, they said they'd forego their trip. My husband reluctantly offered to cancel the week he'd just booked. I asked all of them to wait until we'd looked at all the options before we decided what to do. We intended to drive to Whistler. There had to be more than those two basic alternatives to work with.

My spouse and I spent *10 minutes* that afternoon generating ideas. Then we called the kids back and suggested the following options:

- Cancel our trip and stay home with the baby.

- Have the kids stay home from their trip

- Take the baby with us on our trip for the week

- Take the baby with us, but have baby's mom drive up and get him once they returned from their trip (which was only going to be four days).

- Take the baby and have Mom drive up and join us for the rest of the week once they returned from their trip.

The last two ideas took things in a really cool direction. Baby's daddy objected to being left out. He had vacation days available and had always wanted to see Whistler. They would both come up and join us once they returned from their trip. The solution we ended up with gave us far more than the obvious solutions we'd begun with. It was special shared family time we would not have gotten otherwise.

Here Come Da Judge

The joke about good judgment is true: You develop good judgment by gaining experience, and you gain experience by exercising poor judgment. At least when we are looking at retirement, we are pretty far along that learning curve. That's good because now we need to know when to judge and when to withhold judgment, when to make things happen, when to let things happen, and when to wait until things happen on their own.

Carefully measured decisions have always been considered the hallmark of a decision well made. Kepner Tregoe has been selling this approach for over 40 years. But in his landmark book *Blink*, Malcolm Gladwell lists instance after instance where the ability to make good split-second decisions is the difference between success and failure. He also points out that the quality and validity of the assumptions being used is key to whether those "snap judgments" allow you to soar or cause a crash.

The assumptions we make about the world around us and our place in it help us order our lives. But it's critical that we test these assumptions regularly, particularly when making key decisions. For example, are you assuming your spouse will love to have you home all the time? I remember one retiree wife's retort in particular. "I married you for better or for worse, not for breakfast, lunch, and dinner."

The assumptions we make about what's going to come next after work ends can have disastrous consequences. Fantasies are fun, but if you are going to try to live them, ground them in reality before you start. Check out every single thing you are assuming when you start to make your "after work" plans. If you're married to a guy who hates animals, your dream of running a horse farm is gonna need some work.

INFORMATION QC

At some point in this process, the speed with which you decide to do something major will baffle you. Relax. Much as it looks like it's been done in the blink of an eye, your choice will be the consequence of an on-going process of information gathering and evaluation that pushed you in the right direction almost instantaneously when the right opportunity came along. Don't be afraid of this. It has its place in the corporate world, to be sure. But in personal planning, it's priceless. However, the REAL version only happens when you've been gathering the right information on an on-going basis.

To be useful, your information needs to be current, accurate, and relevant when the opportunity presents itself. Those who start to do their research after an idea unfolds lose traction before they can take advantage of the situation. Those who know what they want and need, what they can afford, where they are trying to go, and what's most important in how they go about their lives can move faster. All sorts of good things come into their lives and they have a lot more fun. Saying "no" is important. But saying "yes" is what it's really about. The more you have done to identify what you want, the easier it's going to be to recognize it when you hear it in the last five words of an ad on the radio or meet a key link at a party.

In the last 10 years, the volume of available information for dealing with any situation has exploded. With a few keystrokes, you can access more data and opinion than you can read on virtually any topic. But volume and quality are not synonymous. As we have gotten more sophisticated at generating information, we seem to have gotten less capable of evaluating it and using it well.

There are four aspects to good information: accuracy, validity of source, freshness, and relevance. Good decision makers put their information through these four screens on an on-going basis.

Accuracy is more difficult to ascertain today than before the Internet. On a computer screen, things look terribly legitimate. In addition, the proliferation of television and online news channels has diluted the likelihood that what is being reported is accurate. The scramble for viewers and our obsession with real time information make it less likely those reporting have done all the checking needed to assure accuracy. We can't even be sure of venerable newspapers any more.

You can use the old "triangulation rule" for the critical stuff: If you find it in three independent places (who did not rely on each other for the information), it's probably true. But that's time consuming, to put it mildly. There are some web sources for checking things out. My former neighbor in Omaha, who works at the library, always goes to *truthorfiction.com* before she passes anything along. Wouldn't it be great if everyone did that.

But to deal with the horrendous volume of information we are flooded with every day without doing these two things means you have to learn who to trust. Automatically ask this question when new information from a new source arrives: How confident am I that this piece of information is legitimate, accurate, and current? If you aren't, don't bother to keep it—in your mind, your magazine rack, or your computer files.

Which brings us to source. Where you get the information makes a huge difference in how much stock you should be placing in it. EVERY-THING that comes to you in an e-mail should be faced with skepticism. Most of what you get with friends dining out, during golf games, and at parties also falls in this category. I've had someone—who thought she was stating the truth—tell me the "crust" over Mount Rainier was really only an inch thick and that it could cave in any day. I've had graduate school friends insist North Dakota is located above Montana. Being smart or pursuing advanced education doesn't mean the person knows what he's talking about in every case.

Consider your source as you take in the information. The person who cuts your hair is probably not the best resource about your investment portfolio. Your stockbroker is probably not your go-to gal on where to hike. The bits of validity-challenged information that come in unsolicited via e-mail in particular are the GIGO ("garbage in garbage out") stuff. You don't need to keep them, much less use them. You probably don't even need to read them.

The importance of using well-sourced information is obvious. You are probably telling yourself you always do that. Go back and look at the last decision you made. Did you send out that e-mail chain letter because someone told you it would be bad luck if you didn't? Did you get in the right lane on the highway because everyone else was, only to discover they were all taking an exit you didn't want to take? We rely on what other people are doing to decide what we are going to do far more often than we realize.

Freshness is also critical. The Internet has enhanced our ability to have up-to-the-minute information on everything from the weather in Bemidji, Minnesota to what Microsoft stock closed at. But a website can be obsolete without looking like it. The other night I agreed to go to a meeting with some friends. We checked the website to confirm what time we had to be there. The website *looked* current. The meeting time stated was not. We were a half hour early. That's not a big deal. But it would be if I decided to sell my house and move 2500 miles because of that information.

Last and most important is relevance. The information you need for decisions now isn't the same as the information you've needed to decide what kind of tires to put on the fleet of vehicles you were responsible for on your job. Years ago, when the company offered you a new position in a different city, the relevant information was about schools and what it would take to get the family resettled. Now you might be more worried about whether there's good mountain biking in the area or if a certain kind of acupuncture is available.

This is not new. We were teaching this stuff in a course called "How to Decide" for women in the natural gas industry (to encourage them to pursue non-traditional careers) in the late 1970's. Too often, we don't do this though. Too often, the assumption is that if it's in print, it's legitimate and if it's on the Internet, it's gospel and was updated in the last five working days.

THE OTHER WEB

Having the right network in place will make a significant difference in how easily you can transition into what you want to do next. Your web of contacts and acquaintances will change as you move out of work, but it's shortsighted to let it atrophy. Especially until society creates the resources to utilize the retirement years effectively, your network is going to be your favorite multipurpose tool—your retirement years Leatherman, if you will. Having personal contacts who will use their own networks to help you gain access and will vouch for your skills, abilities, and energy level can open doors that would likely remain locked otherwise.

Just the word "networking" tends to create anxiety for many of us. But there is no way around it. Given the current lay of the land with ageism, who you know is important. How you know them is not so much a matter of both doing the same thing for a living as in both holding each other in high regard. People like to get involved with people they respect. What you decide to do next is going to be with people you think are worth working with, whether you are working for pay or shouldering a community project.

You need something that gives you a broader circle of contacts than the job you are doing now. Or, as Wayne Dyer says, "You can't be what you do, because then when you don't you aren't." Go beyond work contacts *before* you go out the door.

The best example of using a network to propel himself into the next step again and again is my younger son. He works in finance but to a large extent, his network revolves around lacrosse. He played in high school and then as a club sport in college. When it came time to move 600 miles away to take a job in the business sector he'd chosen, he used his lacrosse contacts to help him create a social circle and, of course, to play the game on an organized basis in his new town.

One of the guys on that team had played on a semi-pro basis in Australia, where the sport is gaining popularity. My son decided he needed this same career side-trip and used his lacrosse network to set up his stint as a youth coach and clinic leader in Perth. When he returned after a year of "walkabout," he tapped into the lacrosse network in the Pacific Northwest to find a job back in the field of finance. He even met his wife at a gathering his lacrosse friends invited him to attend. He loves the game, to be sure. But he also had the good sense to create a larger circle of acquaintances than what his job alone would have provided.

Your network shouldn't just be about what you do. It has to be about who you are. I once helped a friend polish his resume when things weren't going well at the job he was on. He'd met another father at their sons' hockey practice who was looking for project managers. My friend stepped onto that new career path because of his kid's hockey practice. He's been wonderfully successful. He'd have never had the chance if he hadn't taken the time to chat with that other parent while he was watching his kid work on stick skills.

Networking is often misunderstood. It is not a matter of collecting business cards. It is not about how many names you have in your Rolodex or on your PDA. It's about having a shared interest that puts you in contact with people you wouldn't have met otherwise. It's about doing things to help these people when you can—be it moving their furniture when you'd rather be watching the baseball game, letting them know about a job opportunity that just came up where you work, or including them on an art tour you've been invited to attend because you know they are interested.

A network starts with GIVING. And we're not talking about the stuff the company hands out to customers at Christmas either. You pay attention to these people because you like and respect them. They pay attention to you for the same reasons. It's like the symbiotic relationships we learned about in high school biology. As part of the team building sessions in the work setting, it's called Win Win.

A well-established network is priceless in many different ways. It's a source of information, sure. It's also a source of support. It's an early warning system sometimes. And if you are going to change geography, it's an immediate invitation to fun you'd spend months looking for otherwise. Networks might well be THE primary resource for things you want to make happen once you retire. At least in the near term.

Ironically, when we leave work, the network starts to atrophy instantly. Maintaining a strong, vibrant network is probably one of the most important things we can do at this stage of our lives. Usually we do just the opposite, partly because so much of it was tied to work.

When you walk out the door, that kind of network stays behind. Even if you promise you are going to get together for lunch, golf, coffee, or whatever, you lose contact quickly. You NEED a network. Start to broaden it beyond your job now so that when you leave all that behind, the majority of your most important contacts don't even know the difference.

WOO WOO 101

I've never perceived rational thought and intuition as competing options. They're more like a screwdriver and a pliers from the same toolbox.

As a businessperson, rational thought is essential. I was, and am, good at it. It's what you need for driving a car, filing your income taxes, or halving a recipe. Rational thought works well in situations where you are manipulating known facts to reach conclusions and make decisions from them. Rational thought does not work as well when you are working with incomplete or non-rational information.

It also doesn't work when you can't get *to* the rational, factual information. That's why intuition became so important to me as I began to focus on what I liked and didn't like, what I needed more of in my life and what I needed less of. Truth goes far beyond rational thought and can't be contained in it. I discovered that much of what is most true for me could not be accessed via my mind, which stubbornly functions like an overzealous Spam filter way too much of the time.

My truth has to be felt. That involves intuition.

In her book, *Developing Intuition*, Shakti Gawain, describes it as the inner knowing that's part of "a universal, intelligent life force that exists within everyone and everything." Dr. Larry Dossey, in *Reinventing Medicine* suggests that it is nonlocal, that when we rely on intuition, solutions "seem to come from a source of wisdom greater than our own." Much as learning to reach this level of connection with intuitive skills is worthwhile and useful, it's not necessary for what we need to do with it. For our purposes, we will use the same techniques to get to information within ourselves that's buried under a lot of societal clutter and accumulated obsolete information. To chart a good path, you need to know the territory. In this case, the garbage is deep enough—at least for most of us—that learning what's underneath it is easier done with a telemetric tool than digging through all that stuff one piece at a time. That telemetric tool is intuition.

Caroline Myss in *Anatomy of the Spirit* cautions that most of us confuse intuition with prophetic ability. This isn't about being able to pick horses at the track. This is about being able to access the emotional, psychological and spiritual components of a given situation. What we want is to get beyond the facts—or maybe even just through the top layer of them—to better define the overall picture.

All you "Y" chromosome people—listen up! This is not "girls stuff." My dad told me he knew when his youngest sister had died because she stopped by the house as she was leaving. Sounds logical but Aunt Peg lived in Ohio and Dad in Wisconsin. She died hundreds of miles away—in the hospital after a prolonged illness. Dad was *not* a woo woo guy. He was a jock, a blue-collar mill worker, and a WWII infantry sergeant. But he respected his intuition and used it.

My older son, who loves anything that involves a combustion engine and speed, uses his intuition when he drives. He tells stories of accidents he's avoided by listening to his gut. I'm glad the next generation is this proficient. My own experience with intuition on the highway is more that of sensing I've just done something stupid the split second before the highway patrol comes up behind me with the lights flashing.

Developing your "gut instincts" is kind of fun. The biggest challenge is making your rational mind shut down for long enough to play with it without that interference. Gawain offers a series of exercises in her book that are quite helpful. If you don't want to do all that, try at least the following:

1. Think of at least three situations in which you have been willing to listen to your gut instincts. When you did, what happened? When you ignored your hunches, what was the result?

2. The next time you are on the freeway, pay attention to the car in front of you on the right. Try to anticipate when that car is going to do something different—like pull into your lane or take the exit. (BEFORE the turn signal comes on!)

3. Do you know where your gut feel is in your body? What does a hunch feel like physically? Tightness in the chest? A flutter sensation in the solar plexus?

4. Notice and go with your gut feel at least once in the next 24 hours.

Paying attention to intuitive information makes decision making a lot easier. (Edison was intuitive. The idea for the incandescent light bulb came to him in a dream.) But there is also a price for *not* paying attention to it. Many people report feeling depleted or depressed or even numb if they ignore their intuitive urgings. According to Gawain, "There may be a sense of having to push to make things happen." Why do that to yourself? Use your intuition.

Think and Do

Practicing is the only way to get proficient with any tool. I am always surprised at what I learn after I thought I was good at something. So do these exercises even if you think you are a master craftsman with the full set of tools I've just described. At a minimum, you will validate that assumption.

Exercise 2.1—Problems Problems Problems

Describe a problem you currently need to solve: _____

_____

_____

Part 1. Solutions

List all the solutions you can think of for solving it. _____

_____

_____

Let your mind "take a nap" by thinking about a place you find pleasant for a few minutes. When you come back, list any solution ideas that came "while you were gone." _____

_____

_____

Look at the total list. Will anything you've listed make a new, better option if two or more are combined or if parts of several are put together?

_____

_____

_____

_____

Part 2. Consequences

On a scale of 1 to 100, how important is this problem?

NOT AT ALL   EXTREMELY

0   10   20   30   40   50   60   70   80   90   100

What will happen if it isn't solved?_____

_____

_____

Who will be affected and how?_____

_____

_____

What is the dollar cost likely to be of not solving the problem?

_____

_____

_____

Given its level of importance, how much time should be spent solving the problem?_____

_____

_____

How much time have you spent—and will you spend—solving it?

_____

_____

_____

_____

Part 3. Ownership

Is this your problem?   YES___ NO___

Are you responsible for this as part of your job?   YES___ NO___

Are you responsible for it because the person with the problem is incapable of problem solving (too young, too old, in poor health, absent)?

                                                                  YES___ NO___

If this is not your problem, why are you trying to solve it? _____

_____

_____

Part 4. Peripherals

What else do you need to know to make this decision well? (List the major pieces of information at least.) _____

_____

_____

Where are you going to get that information? (List a source for each item needed.) _____

_____

_____

What will you do if it's not available there? _____

_____

_____

When can you get it? Does this mesh with when the decision needs to be made? _____

_____

_____

Some problems can readily be dealt with in a light-hearted manner. Some are too important to be blithe about. You can laugh about what you want to do tonight. But if there is a negative cash flow situation going on, joking about it won't feel right. Some solutions listed might border on the ridiculous. Don't eliminate them or edit them before you ever write them down. There have been times when the wacky idea morphed and morphed again and eventually became "the perfect solution."

The lesson in this exercise is about taking the time to generate options and identify what you need to know and where you can get that information. Yes. It's very tempting to run with the first thing we think of, with only half of the information we need. But these are important decisions and we don't want to end up dealing with another problem that was created by the first solution.

The amount of time spent on a decision should be in proportion to the importance of the decision being made. I would spend a lot more time figuring out how to improve family cash flow than dealing with neighbors who are raising chickens when it's prohibited.

Other people's problems that you are asked to play a role in solving need to be recognized for what they are—not yours. If the person with the problem is a competent adult, solving it for him/her denies that person the chance to demonstrate competence. Be careful with that. There are a lot of grown children whose parents are still helping them, not because they can't do it, but because Mom and Dad never got used to the idea that they could.

As a side note, there are also decisions to be made about helping with solutions other people define for their problems. If it isn't yours, you don't *have* to fix it. Just because someone else has concluded that your doing something is the best way to solve his/her problem doesn't mean you have an obligation to do that. Don't do stuff for other people that robs you of the time and resources you need to get on with your own life. Unless, of course, you really *want* to do it.

Exercise 2.2—The Good, the Bad, and the Ugly

Evaluate the quality of the following information… 1 = poor; 9 = excellent

	accuracy	relevance	validity	freshness
An article of interest in today's newspaper	____	____	____	____
Information on stocks from your welfare uncle	____	____	____	____
A 1989 book on estate planning	____	____	____	____
User's manual for the 1957 Chevy you're restoring	____	____	____	____
The current USGA Rules Book (golf)	____	____	____	____
Your sister's blog	____	____	____	____
A stock guru's blog	____	____	____	____

The quality of information you acquire is a function of what you are trying to do with it. If you are restoring a 1957 Chevy, a 1957 user's manual will be a whole lot more valuable than the current version or than the one for 1977.

The qualifications of the person providing the information will help in assessing its likely quality. The uncle with no investment training or experience is far less likely to have good information than the financial guru who writes a blog. But if your uncle has picked winners for the family nine years out of the last ten, his track record makes his recommendations relevant.

Relevance is a direct function of use. If you don't play golf, even a rulebook so current the ink is still drying will not be relevant for you. If this source of information has been on target in the past for what you are trying to do, using it again is a no-brainer. But it is very easy to be taken in by things that look official and sound relevant these days. The Internet makes this assessment much harder because of the veil of anonymity that e-commerce and e-mail create. This is another place where trusting your gut can add to your success. If it feels wrong, it probably is. Don't get into it.

Freshness is for more than fruit. How current your information is does make a difference. The most extreme examples are in the second to second changes in a trading pit. But it's true for things as straightforward as deciding where you are going to go for a hike. The ten o'clock news last night isn't going to be as useful as going online or checking the Weather Channel just before you head out in the morning.

My first date ever with a millionaire (when it still meant something...) netted the following advice: *Never make a decision before it's time to.* If you do, you're using less than the most recent information. I had, up to that point, been doing just that, just to keep ahead of all that was going on in my job and my life. His advice saved me many a headache professionally even if things didn't click romantically.

One last note about information gathering. Don't collect information you aren't going to use. Eventually, you will drown in it. Knowing how to get what you are looking for when you need it is far more effective.

Exercise 2.3—Realms of possibility

List all the different groups where you have contacts and friends. Draw lines between the ones that would be likely to interact with each other.

_____

_____

_____

_____

_____

_____

_____

This work helps you see whether you have much "stretch" in your network. If everyone already knows everyone, then you will have a harder time using them to gain access to new resources when you need them. For example, you may list your church group, your choir mates and your bible study group separately, but they are still pretty much the same group of people.

To give you an idea of what this looks like for someone else, here's my list-of-the-moment and my assessment of how effective this network is.

- Hiking buddies
- Ski club friends
- Women's circle friends
- Friends from Omaha days
- Friends from Colorado Springs days
- Friends from when I worked in Denver
- Friends from the neighborhood I lived in before this one
- Current neighbors
- "The water women" (a trio of friends who like boats)
- The volleyball people
- UP for Art (a nonprofit in which I am involved)
- Screenwriting guild friends, people I've pitched to, UCLA classmates and instructors
- Executive Branding/Masterminds network
- Red Cross acquaintances and associates
- Service providers…stockbroker, hair dresser, landscaper, etc
- Family….here and in Wisconsin
- My writing group

The strength of my list is in its diversity. Most of these people don't know each other or at least don't circulate in the same places. It's weak in terms of giving me access to what I need now though. It's short on professional contacts. And since all of the above are a function of where I've been or what I've done before, they aren't on target with what I want to do next.

As I learn more about "the next thing," I'll build a network that more directly attaches to things of interest in the new direction. But I wish I could have stayed more connected to the people I knew in the natural gas business. At an industry conference a few years before I left, my boss told me "You know more people than God." Not anymore. And I wish I'd done that differently. They were fun, kind, and made my life better.

How about your list? Any surprises? What are you pleased with? What do you want to work on? Is most of it work related? Family? Church? The more variety you have, the better it will serve you and you will serve it. And that is what networking is all about. Give and take.

Exercise—2.4

List five ways to experiment with your intuition. (Aw, come on. Try it.)

1._____

_____

2._____

_____

3._____

_____

4._____

_____

5._____

_____

*A bit daunting if you haven't done anything
with your hunches before, right?*

Things I came up with:

1. Predict what the temperature is going to be before I pass the reader board on the bank on my morning walk.

2. Listen for work direction while doing my stretches in the morning. (This gives me amazing help on work projects that I would have never *thought* of.)

3. Predict what song is about to play on the radio. (The *radio*— not a favorite CD whose sequence I have memorized.)

4. Notice, honor and do the things that "come up" that relate to work but aren't things I was consciously trying to make happen.

5. Meditate—in a chair or lying on my back on the floor— and see what comes.

When I do this last thing well, total calm descends around me. If I keep doing it and listen for what's in the void, advice and direction come. I try to journal about that message for a page, which helps flesh it out. If you prefer, you might recall the message when you're stuck in traffic or waiting somewhere. It beats fuming about what's going on around you and helps focus on the real work. Just hold the words without passing judgment on them. Often, guidance will come. But if you want help, you have to let it in. Telling yourself "This is dumb. Why am I doing it?" the whole time you're attempting to meditate is like locking and double bolting the door. Nothing is going to get in if you aren't willing to let it. Meditate without judging the practice beforehand or don't bother.

The first step in accessing your intuition is getting your mind to turn off so you can hear your inner voice. There are guided meditations that start with "Tell your mind to take a nap…." or to send it on vacation. Anything you can do to stop thinking—while awake—makes accessing your intuitive guidance easier.

The next challenge is being comfortable with the silence. Inner knowing is peaceful—not at all like CNN Headline News or a radio talk show. Accessing intuition is calming as well as informative. If you have no experience with this kind of silence, it might take a few tries to get comfortable with it. When you are calm and can hear your own breathing, intuitive messages are more likely to come. Stay open. Be calm. Stop thinking.

There are books of many kinds on meditation. It's not hard to do and doesn't automatically make you part of any particular religion. I got interested in it when a psychiatrist told me it was the only way people could function effectively on less sleep. I was a fulltime employee and graduate student with two young kids and a husband who traveled a lot on his job. I needed all the help I could get.

ON BEYOND THINKING

As a young mom with an infant and a preschooler, I was chatting with my husband and one of the guys he worked with over a beer one night when the friend asked me "What's your favorite thing to do?" Without a second's hesitation, I answered, "Think." Mind you, I'd already discovered sex, good scotch, and semi-sweet chocolate.

Thinking is the ultimate entertainment for me. I was one of those maladjusted kids who loved story problems. My most embarrassing secret in high school was that I liked to take tests. (Still do. Please don't tell my friends.) I don't need music or TV or even a car if I have something fun to think about. You have to understand this. Thinking has been important—*essential*—to me my entire life. I want you to know that because it will help you appreciate the magnitude of the advice I am about to give.

Don't think. At least, not always.

There are times when thinking puts you at a distinct disadvantage.

Sometimes, not thinking makes it easier to say or do something hard. My first lesson in this was as a sophomore in high school when one of my close friends lost her older sister in a car accident. I worried for days over what I could possibly say when I talked with her and her family at the funeral home. Then I finally decided the best thing to do was to say what came into my head at that moment—without thinking. And it worked. It was the right thing to do then. It's been the most effective way to proceed when I've tried to console someone ever since. Why? Because to connect with someone who is grieving, you must inhabit the realm of deep emotion. Rational thought is useless there.

Learning to not think has been a slow process for me. The consequences when I did it randomly were not always stellar. I can remember disappointing my mother one Christmas by blurting out "It's a giant Tootsie Roll!" as my five-year old son started to open a gift from her. I had no idea what was in the package. I'd just let the first thought that entered my head come out of my mouth. It *was* a giant Tootsie Roll. I'd never seen one before. Mom was pretty disgusted with me for ruining her surprise.

Another embarrassing moment in a similar vein came when I was the division manager for a natural gas company in Colorado. We'd planned an elaborate set of funny outdoor games called The Couch Potato Olympics as a way to have some fun at a customer meeting. The Colorado weather didn't cooperate, and we were stuck inside playing Pictionary with flip charts and easels as team competition.

I'd been assigned to a team, but was called away to attend to something as we got started. When I got back, "artists" from both the teams were hard at work on the same word. My teammate had drawn a series of peaks on the chart pack He added a fish as I walked back in. I shouted "New Zealand" from the back of the room. Both artists stopped drawing and stared at me. Stunned silence followed. It was the right answer. I sure hadn't gotten to it with logic.

No one—including me—could believe what had happened. Did it spook me? A little. But I suspect it scared the daylights out of the guy at the easel. My boss told me later that this guy was really worried about how to negotiate "with a woman" and had gone so far as to ask my boss how to go about it. And there I was with "psychic powers."

I tried the same technique a couple months ago on a pack trip—same result, until I started thinking and panicked about making a spectacle of myself by getting them right again and again. Then I started guessing wrong just like everyone else.

I don't really think these things are psychic. I think they are an end run on the limits of the rational mind. Jung called it tapping into the collective unconscious. I call it going with my gut. Whatever it is, it's helped me discover when my kid was playing hooky in high school—more than once—and helped us catch an employee in a diabolically clever embezzlement scheme.

I have since put more effort into tapping and appreciating my intuition. When I realized I was going to have to give up on the marriage, access to my intuition saved my sanity. Whenever the panic of so much change and uncertainty at once started to get to me, I would go quiet and listen to my breathing. From there I could see what I needed to focus on and then I was fine.

There are a few stories that are farther out. But telling them isn't what this book warrants. I have found that I make much better decisions about what to do with my life when I use all the skills in the toolbox. Intuition included. I hope you at least experiment with it before you decide whether you will, too.

Chapter Three:

Combing Your
Personal Beach

WHEN I WAS IN EIGHTH GRADE, the company my dad worked for wanted him to move to New Milford, Connecticut to help start a new mill. This threw the entire family into a dither. Leave everything we knew? Move a thousand miles away and start from scratch?

I was heartily in favor of the proposition. It would be an instant remedy for everything I didn't like about my life. Moving to New Milford would make me popular. My skin would be clear. I'd be beautiful. I'd have really cool clothes. I'd be the girl all the boys wanted to talk to. Just packing up my bedroom was going to make me able to handle any social situation with grace and skill. The uncool, awkward me would no longer be part of the equation. She would stay in Wisconsin.

We didn't move.

Dad had a heart condition, and his doctor didn't think it was a good idea. So I had to go from ugly duckling to swan the hard way. I would have had to anyway, so it's good I didn't move across the country to find that out.

The idea that retiring from your current job is going to make life instantly perfect is just as unrealistic. The change may be the best thing you ever did, but it will still require adjustments. Some things won't work out quite as well as you expected. There will be gaps and lumps and bare spots. Seamless transitions are rare. That's probably good for most of us. Where's the fun in an instant success?

People who make life's transitions well tend to do better because they look at them realistically. They're the Boy Scouts—prepared. They know their strengths, interests, and weaknesses. They have some sense of the territory they're entering and the challenges it will engender. They've thought about how to mesh their own uniqueness and the specific world they've just bought a ticket to enter.

So how do you get a handle on all this? Odd as it sounds, you have to take the time to understand who you are. Seems we should know that by now, given the number of years we've been at it. Usually, the opposite is true. We've been accommodating various situations for so long and with such regularity that who we really are at our core has gone dormant.

Dormant. Not dead. And not just stuff stored in the really ancient lockers of childhood and youth. Who you are now does include that stuff. But ignoring the current parts is just as ineffective as failing to consider the old delights. So…what are you good at? What do you like? What have you learned you need to avoid to live a happy life? Where are your interests turning these days? How are you spending the discretionary time you already have? The answers to these questions usually aren't just sitting out there where you can find them in an instant. Think about them. Maybe while you are mowing the lawn (or shoveling the walk). Maybe while you are commuting or waiting for someone who's running late.

You may not need to go back to what you liked to do when you were five. (Your intuition will tell you if that would be useful.) You do have to do a good inventory of what's really you now. And that includes the contexts you're enmeshed in—what's going on in the world you participate in every day. With all that figured out, defining a satisfying lifestyle for yourself should be cake. Well, at least a *recipe* for cake.

This chapter looks at the elements that contribute to a lifestyle. *Think and Do* will pop up throughout the chapter instead of all in one place because focusing on each aspect completely and then moving on is easier. Since this is your first pass at gathering information, a lot of it should be on the surface and fairly easy to access. But sometimes that is more as a teaser than a total find. These "information expeditions" are like field exploration in mining. Often, they simply provide the insight to know where it will be most productive to come back and dig deeper later.

A life has many facets and how these facets are addressed defines a lifestyle. Your job is just the start. If you're going to do this well—and I hope I have made a case for that in the last two chapters—then you will also want to take stock of your family situation, social circle, consumer habits, physical and mental health, personal preferences, and spiritual satisfaction as you consider what you want to do next.

One last thing. Sometimes what's perceived as dissatisfaction in one arena is really a problem with some other area of life. Often, work dissatisfaction masks primary relationship issues. Fury with what a neighbor is doing could be the tip of an entirely different iceberg. We humans like to play games with ourselves. So don't assume it's all about that one obvious, impossible aspect of your life.

All the Live Long Day

When we are unhappy, the vast majority of us blame "the job." In particular, we think that working full time is the problem. Work is an essential part of feeling effective as a human being. The paycheck is optional, but we all need to feel like we are making a difference. Most of us *must* work, sometimes for the money, but just as often for the mental challenge, the social interaction, or the sense of competence and contribution that work provides. But we also need to have control over *how much* we work so we have room for the other things we want in our lives. So let's assume there is likely to be something in your new life on which you expend effort to make something happen—work.

The Merrill Lynch study reported that only six percent of all the baby boomers who want to work after retirement—over three quarters of that population—want to work full time. This is the case even though many of us want to start new careers. Clearly, the paradigm must shift here.

There is work to do that those leaving the workforce are best at. We need to find ways to allow them to do that work without having to show up all day everyday.

But is this work, *your* work now?

Do you like it?

Do you like the work you're doing currently? Is the work itself fulfilling? Stimulating? A source of excitement more often than not? This is the most important aspect of work to look at when you have the chance to leave it behind. Perhaps you've been in the same line of work for decades. Does it still suit you? If you've already retired from it, do you miss doing this work specifically?

If you enjoy the work you do, don't walk away from it entirely. Leaving it behind when it gives you satisfaction is denying yourself part of your customized good life. Incorporating the way you use your expertise differently may be far more rewarding.

The generations moving into the workforce as the baby boom leaves have fewer workers available. Business magazines and think tanks are already warning of skilled labor shortages and an "experience drain." Phased retirement is one way to keep some of this expertise longer. Twenty-five percent of the companies surveyed by the Society for Human Resource Management allow workers old enough to retire to continue their employment on customized terms, such as reduced hours. Another 24 percent of the companies surveyed are planning to introduce this kind of program.

But a study of corporations done by Ernst & Young and the Human Capital Institute found more than 85 percent of the companies who responded had no formal retention programs for the expertise getting ready to retire. That seems to contradict what the SHRM study found, but perhaps not. The conclusion that corporate America is "facing a significant wisdom withdrawal" may be a bit overstated. This is new terrain for all concerned. As a valued employee reaches the point where leaving is feasible, the arrangements made to retain his/her expertise are not likely to be part of a thoroughly designed program. The response to the prospect of losing key knowledge and skill will be a problem solving effort unique to that situation—not a formal program. At least not until this has been going on for a decade or two.

The employee who understands his/her own value and has taken the time to clarify preferences and desired lifestyle is quite likely to negotiate a better arrangement *without* a formal program. Eventually, there will be specific plans in place to do such things, but for now, we're going to have to roll our own. This is good.

Much as negotiating something with the outfit you are currently working for is probably the easiest way to keep your hand in what you are doing, that doesn't mean it's always best. If you don't respect your current employer, like the work but not how you are being allowed to do it, or just plain don't like the work anymore, do walk away from the current situation totally when you retire. If you have no choice—the work went away, the company is going away, whatever—or if you've already retired and are now looking for new options, fear not. This is where you get to do it your way anyway. After you figure out what that is.

The extent to which variety is part of your make-up is also an important factor here. If you have done the same thing since you got out of school and loved it, sticking to that area of expertise makes sense. But if you've already had several careers and have gone in a new direction every few years throughout your work years, expecting you're going to want to do the same thing for the rest of your life is silly.

There is also a case for developing the opposite side of ourselves at this point. If the bills are covered via retirement income, what you do "for a living" doesn't have to demand the same level income. You can do it for the love of it without starving to death. Going in the opposite direction is okay here. If you've been focused on logic and facts and want to move toward a more creative kind of life, go for it! Carol Lloyd (no relation) wrote *Creating a Life Worth Living* to help with this kind of transition.

If you've been a creative for 40 years, don't think you've lost it if doing something analytical suddenly appeals. If you've been a paper-pushing professional, it might be time to bloom using your hands. Notice your day dreams. Those niggling little ideas that don't go away mean your heart is trying to get your attention. You can do whatever you want with your time now. Make it exciting and fun and what gives you joy.

A *Smart Money* article suggests there are really three phases we will go through as retirees: Retiring to Work, The Wonder Years, and Watching the Sunset. Their contention is the first third of the years after full time work will still involve work, the next third will involve the travel and exploration often perceived as "retirement" now, and the final third will be winding down to death.

I'm not at all convinced our lives will fall into these nice neat bands. Life is messy. It's likely we'll move back and forth between the three lifestyles they described many times during these years. Perhaps an injury or illness, or taking time to care for an aging parent will leave you "watching sunsets" for a few years after which you decide to start a web-based business or launch a motivational speaking career. Work could easily be a part of all three phases. And the questions to be answered about work are:

- What would be fun?
- Do I need to get paid for it?
- Can I do it in smaller doses than 8 to 5?

Think and *Do*

Exercise 3.1 — WORK

How much do you enjoy the work you're doing now? Consider each dimension and mark your current situation to give yourself a look. If you are already retired, think in terms of what you're doing with your time regardless of whether it involves pay.

NOT AT ALL					SOMETIMES					TOTALLY
0	10	20	30	40	50	60	70	80	90	100

The work I am doing interests me.

NOT AT ALL					SOMETIMES					TOTALLY
0	10	20	30	40	50	60	70	80	90	100

I feel I am making an important contribution with what I do.

NOT AT ALL					SOMETIMES					TOTALLY
0	10	20	30	40	50	60	70	80	90	100

I like the kinds of projects I work on and what I get to do.

NOT AT ALL					SOMETIMES					TOTALLY
0	10	20	30	40	50	60	70	80	90	100

I'd rather be doing this work somewhere else.

NOT AT ALL					SOMETIMES					TOTALLY
0	10	20	30	40	50	60	70	80	90	100

I'd rather be doing something totally different.

NOT AT ALL					SOMETIMES					TOTALLY
0	10	20	30	40	50	60	70	80	90	100

If I couldn't do <u>this</u> work, I would want to stop working entirely.

NOT AT ALL					SOMETIMES				TOTALLY	
0	10	20	30	40	50	60	70	80	90	100

I miss my work when I don't get to do it.

NOT AT ALL					SOMETIMES				TOTALLY	
0	10	20	30	40	50	60	70	80	90	100

I don't like the company I work for.

NOT AT ALL					SOMETIMES				TOTALLY	
0	10	20	30	40	50	60	70	80	90	100

I wish I'd trained for a different line of work.

NOT AT ALL					SOMETIMES				TOTALLY	
0	10	20	30	40	50	60	70	80	90	100

The work I do has become boring.

If you love it, find a way to keep it in your life in some form.
If you are tired of it, it may be time to move on.

ALL IN THE FAMILY

What do you have going with the family? Certain family situations are not good times to change everything around. Be honest. Would your retirement create instability the family as a whole can't afford? Conversely, is your continuing to work creating challenges? Are you still raising kids? Are you an empty nester? A silver single? The situation at home is important to consider. And part of that consideration has to be whether you LIKE what is going on at home.

Achy breaky Billy Ray Cyrus's advice to his daughter about her acting career is probably just as apt here. "If you ain't having fun, it ain't working." Many of us lead quietly desperate lives at home, telling ourselves it's not worth the effort it would take to make it change. Some of us try to change it and can't. Some of us gave up expecting it to be enjoyable a long time ago. All too often home becomes a matter of territory. She rules the kitchen.

He holds the garage. She uses the upstairs, he the down. The living room is the demilitarized zone where everyone gathers for polite conversation when the kids or friends come to visit. Retiring into this is lunacy.

It's also nuts to retire into a duet that has all the excitement of dried mud. Home needs to be a good place. The people you come home to need to be happy to see you—and you them. Pretense in this arena can continue if you make it—at least for a while. But the body-mind link is strong. Dissatisfaction with your primary relationship really can make you sick.

This is probably the least addressed topic of how to retire well—what to do if the situation at home is "iffy." This isn't about who's right and who's wrong. The question is whether it's working and what to do if it's not.

It's not within the scope of what we're doing here to delve into relationship issues in detail. However, Mira Kirshenbaum does in *Too Good to Leave, Too Bad to Stay.* Using case histories from her own counseling practice, she describes various relationship scenarios and relates whether others in that situation found staying or leaving to be most effective. I'm not advocating either one. I am suggesting you admit what's really there. If the thought of going home at the end of the day makes you ponder finding a bridge to jump off—or hoping your spouse has, retiring to spend 24/7 in that environment is not going to be satisfying. It probably won't be healthy either.

One particularly lethal version of this problem is verbal abuse. This kind of abuse is not about who has the bigger biceps. Both men and women can be subjected to verbal abuse and are. Verbal abuse isn't always the insult-slinging hot rage we typically envision either. The most insidious kind is cold—where someone destroys your self-esteem and potentially your sanity by not letting you be who you are in diabolically subtle ways.

This kind of person is good at convincing you that what she wants is really what you want. She'll tell you, in sweet tones, that everything is fine—because it is for her—when you've just brought up a problem she's creating that you can no longer endure. When you try to improve a situation, she might play along, but nothing really changes for the better. When a "perfect couple" files for divorce after decades, this could well have been going on. Cold verbal abusers come across as very nice people to society in general. To the couple's social circle. To their kids and other family members. Getting away from a cold verbal abuser is difficult because she will make you think you are the one being unreasonable and the loved ones you look to for support are likely to agree.

The Verbally Abusive Relationship by Patricia Evans gives more detail about this difficult challenge. Accept this reality if it's yours. It is not going to change simply because you pretend it isn't there. Please believe me. You need to do something about this if you want to live the rest of your life happy—or even reasonably satisfied.

Even when the person you are living with is loving, kind, and all the things that we want them to be, there are times when the conversation doesn't go anywhere near where you need it to go. Harriet Lerner's *The Dance of Connection* provides excellent help in dealing with those kinds of situations more effectively.

Spouses are not the only issue on the home front. Are you supporting adult children? Are you caring for an infirm parent? Are there things that go on at your house all day when you aren't there—like a daycare or bridge club—that are going to make being there very different than when you get home after work? What will the situation be when home is the only place you have to go to?

Exercise 3.2 — HOME

Same drill. Mark the scales to describe what home is like now for you:

NOT AT ALL   SOMETIMES   TOTALLY

| 0 | 10 | 20 | 30 | 40 | 50 | 60 | 70 | 80 | 90 | 100 | N/A |

My home is my refuge; I relax as soon as I walk in the door.

NOT AT ALL   SOMETIMES   TOTALLY

| 0 | 10 | 20 | 30 | 40 | 50 | 60 | 70 | 80 | 90 | 100 | N/A |

I am not married but wish I were.

NOT AT ALL   SOMETIMES   TOTALLY

| 0 | 10 | 20 | 30 | 40 | 50 | 60 | 70 | 80 | 90 | 100 | N/A |

My spouse helps me meet my needs and supports me emotionally.

NOT AT ALL   SOMETIMES   TOTALLY

| 0 | 10 | 20 | 30 | 40 | 50 | 60 | 70 | 80 | 90 | 100 | N/A |

My kids handle their own affairs and don't need me to solve their problems.

NOT AT ALL   SOMETIMES   TOTALLY

| 0 | 10 | 20 | 30 | 40 | 50 | 60 | 70 | 80 | 90 | 100 |

I am comfortable at home no matter what is going on.

NOT AT ALL   SOMETIMES   TOTALLY

| 0 | 10 | 20 | 30 | 40 | 50 | 60 | 70 | 80 | 90 | 100 |

When I am home, I feel lonely even when others are there.

NOT AT ALL   SOMETIMES   TOTALLY

| 0 | 10 | 20 | 30 | 40 | 50 | 60 | 70 | 80 | 90 | 100 |

I don't like the living arrangement I have now.

NOT AT ALL   SOMETIMES   TOTALLY

| 0 | 10 | 20 | 30 | 40 | 50 | 60 | 70 | 80 | 90 | 100 |

The only reason I am in my relationship is the kids.

NOT AT ALL					SOMETIMES				TOTALLY	
0	10	20	30	40	50	60	70	80	90	100	N/A

The only reason I am in my relationship is it's better than having no one.

NOT AT ALL					SOMETIMES				TOTALLY	
0	10	20	30	40	50	60	70	80	90	100

I like being away from home more than being home.

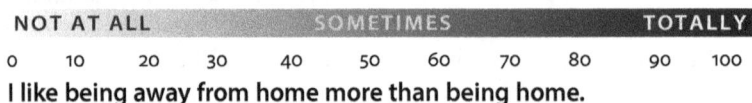

These are just test wells. If any of these scales made you uneasy, write a page or more about how you feel about your situation. As you do so, remember you are the only one you can change. If things aren't working, admit that at least part of it—and most likely all of it—will be up to you to remedy. Think in terms of things you can do yourself. It isn't always about leaving. But it is always about changing: "If you keep doing what you're doing, you'll keep getting what you're getting."

THE SOCIAL WHIRL

Friends are every bit as important as family, often more so. Many of us no longer have the nuclear families we grew up in when we reach this part of our lives. Friends have been playing those roles for years for some of us. But often, what we do with our social time is not well correlated with who we value as friends. This is particularly true if you are a "joiner." Involvement in social organizations can become a form of prison unless it's done with ongoing awareness. Tell me you've never heard someone lamenting he didn't have time to do something he really wanted to do because he had a whole slew of obligations to a fraternal organization, social group, or church community. (We will talk about church in the spiritual sense later.)

Groups take you in and expect you to remain who you were when you joined. When you grow, they don't know what to do with you. Eventually, you will either revert to your old ways to fit in or be pushed out of the group. Caroline Myss outlines this well in *Anatomy of the Spirit*. If you are a member of every organization who will have you, you are probably not the *real* you most of the time.

But we are social creatures, and belonging is one of our primary motivators as humans. As you shape the life you want, take a good long look at what kind of groups are a good fit for you. If you are highly competent and expect work assignments based on being able to get the job done well, spending a large portion of your time volunteering for an organization that prizes seniority will result in frustration all around.

The demands of work often steal the time we'd like for groups we enjoyed belonging to in the past. As we look toward retirement, we may plan on taking up those roles again—but are we the same people we were when they were fun before? Even if friends are sure their group is "perfect" for you, assess it for yourself.

Doing a good job of joining is one of the ultimate balance points of a well-defined lifestyle. You need enough social involvement to feel like you belong but not so much that you are limited to playing only the roles the various organizations require of you.

Friends and a social circle are part of a well-balanced life. However, in a study reported in the American Sociological Review in June 2006, Americans admitted to having fewer friends than when polled in 1985—two now compared to three then. This general trend does not bode well for those leaving the workforce. Quite often, we make friends, if not keep them all our lives, in the workplace. As we leave that fertile ground behind, we need a clear idea of how we are going to replace those friendships with ones that are consistent with the new lifestyle.

Exercise 3.3—THE SOCIAL CIRCLE

Third verse. Mark the scales to describe what your social circle is like now:

NOT AT ALL   SOMETIMES   TOTALLY

| 0 | 10 | 20 | 30 | 40 | 50 | 60 | 70 | 80 | 90 | 100 |

I am an active member of many organizations.

NOT AT ALL   SOMETIMES   TOTALLY

| 0 | 10 | 20 | 30 | 40 | 50 | 60 | 70 | 80 | 90 | 100 |

Most of my friends are people I work with.

NOT AT ALL   SOMETIMES   TOTALLY

| 0 | 10 | 20 | 30 | 40 | 50 | 60 | 70 | 80 | 90 | 100 |

I believe in all the organizations I belong to.

NOT AT ALL   SOMETIMES   TOTALLY

| 0 | 10 | 20 | 30 | 40 | 50 | 60 | 70 | 80 | 90 | 100 |

I'm proud of being in many organizations.

NOT AT ALL   SOMETIMES   TOTALLY

| 0 | 10 | 20 | 30 | 40 | 50 | 60 | 70 | 80 | 90 | 100 |

I have many friends but don't belong to groups.

NOT AT ALL   SOMETIMES   TOTALLY

| 0 | 10 | 20 | 30 | 40 | 50 | 60 | 70 | 80 | 90 | 100 |

I'm not interested in having friends.

NOT AT ALL   SOMETIMES   TOTALLY

| 0 | 10 | 20 | 30 | 40 | 50 | 60 | 70 | 80 | 90 | 100 |

I am more of a networker than a joiner. I know lots of people but to get things done rather than to "belong."

NOT AT ALL   SOMETIMES   TOTALLY

| 0 | 10 | 20 | 30 | 40 | 50 | 60 | 70 | 80 | 90 | 100 |

Being part of a social group is over-rated. I'd rather stay home.

NOT AT ALL					SOMETIMES			TOTALLY		
0	10	20	30	40	50	60	70	80	90	100

I miss the kind of friendships I had as a kid and want to build those in retirement.

NOT AT ALL					SOMETIMES			TOTALLY		
0	10	20	30	40	50	60	70	80	90	100

I keep in touch with friends from my childhood, school and former jobs.

My ideal lifestyle in terms of social situations would be:

_____

_____

_____

Most of us need friends. They make us laugh, keep us honest, and help us with the everyday challenges of living. They also get us in trouble, create havoc with what we were going to do with a Saturday, and help us go off a diet. Friends are the salt and pepper of life. Things just aren't as tasty alone.

Each of us is different in terms of how much and what kind of socializing is optimal. Don't join because your spouse wants you to. Don't avoid someone interesting because they are not currently in any of the groups to which you belong. Create your circle consciously. Keep those you want, add new, but don't be afraid to cull the herd if some things aren't a good fit anymore.

Belonging is about connecting. Connecting is one on one. No matter how many groups you choose to belong to, your satisfaction will depend on whether you take the time to be real with the others in the group. Listen. Relate. Get involved in what's going on. Help. That's real belonging.

America is the richest nation on earth. We are also right up there in terms of consumer debt. We do like to spend money—even money we don't have. If you want to keep doing that into retirement, you have two options. Have enough you'll never run out when you retire or do something to make more as part of your strategy.

Of course, the alternative is to develop better spending habits, but far be it from me to spoil the fun.

In his column for the *Wall Street Journal*, Jonathan Clements notes, "Instead of cutting back, most people constantly strive to raise their standard of living. They are forever aiming for the better car, the bigger house…only to become quickly dissatisfied." He goes on to relate that academics have dubbed this the "hedonic treadmill." We buy, then the thrill of purchasing dissipates and we need to buy something else to recreate it, causing a never-ending cycle.

The problem lies in what we are buying. As Mathew Kelly puts it in *The Rhythm of Life*, "You never can get enough of what you really don't need." We don't need more stuff, we need a reason to get up in the morning. We need passion for what we choose to do with the day. Money is a by-product of doing what you love—at least it should be, especially for the last third of your life.

Let's shed some light on another aspect of the money situation that's touchy, too. If you're working so that other people can spend money, stop it. That's called slavery, and we fought a war almost 150 years ago to eliminate it. Supporting grown kids who can't get their act together is only postponing the inevitable. Someday you are *not* going to be there, and they are going to have to figure it out. If you are working so your spouse can go to the track, the casino, or Nordstrom, you are enabling an addict. Get help and stop doing it.

Even if you had Bill Gates's billions, you might still have trouble with this money thing once you stop earning it actively. For some, spending money is very hard to do, especially when it involves dipping into savings. Even if that is what the money was saved for. If you're that kind of person, keep that in mind as you structure your retirement. You might need something that looks like an "income stream." A part-time job or a consulting gig does that. A Social Security or pension check comes close. But liquidating a stock to meet expenses may give you emotional heartburn. Know who you are. Then have a nice honest chat with yourself when you have to do things you know are likely to bother you.

Exercise 3.4 — MONEY

Same drill. Mark 'em up.

NOT AT ALL					SOMETIMES					TOTALLY
0	10	20	30	40	50	60	70	80	90	100

I have enough money to do what I want for the rest of my life.

NOT AT ALL					SOMETIMES					TOTALLY	
0	10	20	30	40	50	60	70	8090	100	N/A

The people who rely on the money I make MUST rely on me.

NOT AT ALL					SOMETIMES					TOTALLY	
0	10	20	30	40	50	60	70	8090	100	N/A

The people I support make contributions that balance what I earn.

NOT AT ALL					SOMETIMES					TOTALLY
0	10	20	30	40	50	60	70	80	90	100

I am comfortable spending money even when I don't have any coming in.

NOT AT ALL					SOMETIMES					TOTALLY
0	10	20	30	40	50	60	70	80	90	100

I buy things I don't need just because I like buying things.

NOT AT ALL					SOMETIMES					TOTALLY
0	10	20	30	40	50	60	70	80	90	100

I buy things so that people think I am successful.

0   10   20   30   40   50   60   70   80   90   100

I love to shop and rarely come home empty-handed.

My attitude toward money is:

_____

_____

_____

_____

My biggest money challenge in retirement will be (or is):

_____

_____

_____

_____

A solution I might choose that would create other problems is:

_____

_____

_____

_____

A better solution might be:

_____

_____

_____

_____

THE BODY IN QUESTION

The prevailing societal attitude is that by the time you hit your 60's you're worn out, dried up, and full of prescription medicine. You need a luxury car, a cruise, and a good financial planner to live the good life. I must be living on another planet because my friends are not like this at all.

I hike eight or more miles in the mountains every Wednesday all summer long with a group whose average age is about 69. These people regularly go abroad to do equally strenuous things when they travel. My ski club is "mature." That is a lot different than "sedate." Many of them still fall in the "maniac" category as skiers, including the drinking part at the end of the day. I have a friend in Texas who's in his 60's and officiates high school football every chance he gets—and bikes, skis, and hikes as well. These are real people. *They* are the people I want to be like.

This idea that we are all falling apart is convenient to a culture obsessed with youth. Linda Ellerbee, television producer, author, and journalist put it well in an editorial she did for *AARP* when she turned 60. She admitted she'd been allowing the young to define "old." The young don't know anything about it—they haven't gotten that far. What's really going on is so far different from what the media and the magazine ads have been depicting. Why are we—or at least most of this culture—willing to believe their baloney?

Helen Harkness advises that much of what we assume as fact about physical aging is actually social conditioning. The focus in the media and in gerontology as a profession has been on the 6 to 15 percent of elders who are frail and ill. The rest of us don't need to go to the doctor, so there's little information about us for them to assess. She cites a series of studies that looked at whether older people could take up a new sport. Those 60 years old or older learned the new skills as quickly as the group of 20-year olds they were compared to. Older adults who walked 30 minutes a day six times a week were 43 percent less likely to die than their couch potato friends.

That doesn't mean you personally are ready to train for a triathlon. But this is an area where you need to go beyond what is assumed to be reality. We do not all need little purple pills (or blue ones). We don't need Depends; we need gear. As we carve out time for more of what we want in our lives, we take to bikes, kayaks, and trails in ever greater numbers. And we look good when we do that with our free time. Looking good gives your self-esteem a boost. And that helps your immune system. Don't tell the pharmaceutical companies. If we all learn to go take a hike, their profits will plummet.

Do be realistic about where you are now. But don't assume that it's all down hill from here. When I was in my 20s, I was diagnosed as having irritable bowel syndrome. In my 30s they added fibromytosis—an early label for the chronic fatigue stuff. In my 40s it was shingles. Then I started listening better—to my heart, my soul, my intuition. My body was reacting to stress not to getting older.

I don't have any of that stuff to deal with anymore. I use a steroid nasal spray when the pollen count gets super high. Other than that, I don't need prescription drugs. Ibuprofin after an afternoon of volleyball may be wise, but I'm essentially drug free. I'm not unique. Another friend of mine, who's 68, was bummed because the doctor wanted him to go on a cholesterol-reducing drug on a trial basis. He doesn't rely on any prescription meds at all. Articles about older people who don't need prescription drugs are finally starting to appear in print.

The BIG issue in terms of health is stress. I have been studying the phenomenon we now point to as the boogeyman since 1977. Research pioneer Hans Selye defined two kinds of stress in his work. Yes, there is a GOOD kind. And sometimes, the thing that creates health challenges is the lack of stress. Kites rise against the wind. A story is only good if there is conflict in it. This idea that no one should ever have to deal with anything difficult is Grade A hogwash. How are you going to develop a good set of emotional muscles without some heavy lifting?

Stress is an *inside* job. Some people die in cushy corporate offices on Monday mornings because of it while people in the Sudan endure outrageous hardship and survive. Stress is not what's happening *to* you. It's what you're doing about what's happening. So before you assume all your stress will instantly disappear once you give up work, take a good long look at what you are doing to generate it in the first place. It definitely will go away in the work context. But will it pop up somewhere else?

Getting to know yourself takes time and effort. Doing a thorough, honest inventory of who you are now gives you solid foundation for everything from here on. If your job is consuming you and you live in Stress City, consider taking yourself away for a day or two to work on where the stress is actually coming from. Retreats are not always religious endeavors and spas are not just for massages.

The prevailing attitude toward stress—that it's someone else's fault—ties with the current mental health epidemic Caroline Myss calls "victimology." Being a victim has been "in" for several decades now. Victim status means you don't have to be responsible for yourself. You've been "done onto" and should, therefore, be taken care of by the rest of society. We lionize victims way too often. It's awful that the terrible thing happened, but wallowing in it just keeps you from living well once the opportunity returns. The Japanese proverb, "Fall down seven times; stand up eight." is a better plan for life. Bad things happen. Keep going.

Anger is another place where we tend to get off in the weeds. Anger is not good or bad. It is an emotion, an indicator that something is going on—sort of like the burner on the stove getting red when you turn it on. It's what you do with the anger that decides your mental health. Don't retire angry. You will make yourself and everyone around you miserable. If there's work to do in that area, get it done before you go out the door.

Exercise 3.5—HEALTH

And again. Mark the scales in terms of your physical status.

NOT AT ALL					SOMETIMES				TOTALLY	
0	10	20	30	40	50	60	70	80	90	100

I have the physical stamina and strength to do anything physical I want.

NOT AT ALL					SOMETIMES				TOTALLY	
0	10	20	30	40	50	60	70	80	90	100

My fitness level keeps me energized and able to keep going all day.

NOT AT ALL					SOMETIMES				TOTALLY	
0	10	20	30	40	50	60	70	80	90	100

I only go to the doctor for annual exams and check-ups. I'm rarely sick.

NOT AT ALL   SOMETIMES   TOTALLY

| 0 | 10 | 20 | 30 | 40 | 50 | 60 | 70 | 80 | 90 | 100 |

In terms of family history, I will be active and healthy well into old age (90 or beyond).

NOT AT ALL   SOMETIMES   TOTALLY

| 0 | 10 | 20 | 30 | 40 | 50 | 60 | 70 | 80 | 90 | 100 |

My friends consider me a jock.

NOT AT ALL   SOMETIMES   TOTALLY

| 0 | 10 | 20 | 30 | 40 | 50 | 60 | 70 | 80 | 90 | 100 |

I rarely get angry.

NOT AT ALL   SOMETIMES   TOTALLY

| 0 | 10 | 20 | 30 | 40 | 50 | 60 | 70 | 80 | 90 | 100 |

I understand what stresses me and know how to reduce my stress.

My overall physical health is:

_____
_____
_____

My overall fitness level is:

_____
_____
_____

The physical requirements of things I'm thinking about doing in retirement are:

_____
_____
_____

My overall mental health is:

_____
_____
_____

Who Am I Today?

Many of your key aspects of retirement are going to be yours alone. If you enjoy both snow skiing and opera, things aren't going to be too hard to combine. If you want to live in the desert and live on a sailboat, meshing those needs might take a little more creativity.

But then the size of the challenge is important for some of us. Or maybe the amount of competition involved. Or the number of people you can rub elbows with. Or the chance to do your "new work" in the outdoors. Or to work with children…or the disadvantaged…or the elderly. It's really up to you. What's your idea of a fun challenge?

Ten 10's

Before we even get to the official exercise, let's have some fun. If you are having trouble generating information, this is worth the time. If you aren't, your lists may surprise you. If you are trying to do this and 6 other things this afternoon, forget it and just keep reading.

1. List the 10 things that are most important to you in your life.

2. List the 10 people you care most about in the world.

3. List the 10 things you'd do if you only had enough time left in life to do just those ten.

4. List the 10 things you'd enjoy doing most with a free Saturday.

5. List the 10 people you'd most like to meet.

6. List the top 10 places you'd like to see.

7. List the 10 things you'd like most to learn.

8. List the top 10 things you'd like most to do with your life before you die.

9. List the top 10 resources you'd use to get through a difficult time in your life.

10. List the 10 favorite things you'd give away, if it was required, and who you would give them to.

Sort of fun, right? And I'll bet there was stuff that came out that you never expected.

MEGAWATTS

One of the biggies that is often overlooked in retirement planning is energy level. It's important to be aware of it. Energy level is often a surprise once you leave the workplace. That can go either way. For some, losing the burden of the job is like being set free and energy abounds. For others, not having that predictable requirement of how to spend your time is depressing. One of the symptoms of depression is lethargy.

Not being aware of your ideal pace can also create stress. For example, I am extremely high energy and need to do a lot all day to be satisfied. Any less and I don't feel alive. When I was married, I tried to maintain the pace my husband preferred, which was much slower and low key. It was like being sent to jail, but it took me a long time to admit it. If your life partner has a different pace than you, it's not an unavoidable ticket to divorce court. But it is a signal that you two need to have some serious, creative problem-solving discussions.

Exercise 3.6—PAP (Personal Activity Preferences) QUIZ

A true or false test! (I always thought these were the easiest....)
Mark each item according to what is the case most of the time for you:

I like to work alone.	True____	False____
I am the life of the party.	True____	False____
Other people look to me to plan things.	True____	False____
No one keeps things as organized as I do.	True____	False____

I could not care less if my surroundings are clean and neat.	True___	False___
I like to make myself work hard even when I play.	True___	False___
Everyone calls me when they need someone to talk to.	True___	False___
I like doing things that have rules.	True___	False___
The hardest thing for me to do is nothing.	True___	False___
People tell me that just looking at my to do list makes them tired.	True___	False___
I like work that keeps me active— don't ask me to ride a desk.	True___	False___
I need to have something to learn every day.	True___	False___
I like complex challenges and need them often.	True___	False___
It's important to me to live in a warm climate when I retire.	True___	False___
Being near the kids and grandkids is a big deal for me.	True___	False___
I am a self-starter and don't need a boss to get the work done.	True___	False___
I am a leader.	True___	False___
Even when I am supposed to be relaxing, I like to stay busy.	True___	False___
I like to be told what to do and how to do it.	True___	False___
I enjoy doing nothing.	True___	False___

There are no right or wrong answers, of course. (You knew I was going to do that, right?) It's just another run at getting to know yourself. Any surprises? Ask your significant other to do this exercise if you are coupled. Any "ah hah's" about you versus your sweetie in these areas?

Spiritual satisfaction shouldn't be delayed until retirement. But if you are still trying to figure it out, taking the time to see where you are on this dimension will be a big help in charting a course. As we mature, we tend to put more stock in matters of the soul. At this point in life, it's common to feel "empty." That does not mean you are defective. It means you are listening.

I wince when people who've just retired tell me they're so busy they can't figure out how they ever had time to work. That "hedonic treadmill" thing that we could afford when there was a paycheck in the picture is often replaced by "terminal busyness" once retired. Some retirees may be doing a lot of things just to feel like they are doing *something*. What the person is doing and what that person believes in has to strongly correlate for the "busyness" strategy to succeed over the long haul.

A hollow feeling when you think about your commitments is usually a good clue that you're not doing things that feed your soul. Excitement makes you lose track of time. "Busyness" makes you look at the clock, worrying about what you've committed to next. For some, the number of commitments in a week is a way of counting coup. Be careful of that. How much you do is not as important as how good it makes you feel to do it.

The driver needs to be passion. Passion flows from meaning. If you know why you are here and what you believe in, doing things that resonate from those twin beacons will make your life a dream. But let us not kid ourselves here. If you've spent half a century doing what was needed to make money, figuring out what you need to do to make meaning is going to take some effort.

We will revisit the spiritual component later, but for now, it's important to at least begin the process of determining what lights your fire.

Exercise 3.7—Spiritual Satisfaction

Right now, the level of meaning in my life is:

_____

_____

_____

When I look at my calendar I:

_____

_____

_____

Three things I believe very strongly are:

1._____

2._____

3._____

THE MIBBLE RENDITION

Okay, let's take this for a test drive. Mibble…that's me—MBL. This is what I can say about myself after doing some sleuthing in these areas. After you read mine, see what you can come up with for yourself as a summary if you have the time.

I need more work than I have. And I need more structure to it, much as I don't want to admit that. It's too easy to excuse myself from writing because there is no one expecting me to do it. I like to write and write well, but doing it needs to have more of a consequence than it has now. I also need to have more variety in the work I do. I *must* write—any writer will tell you that's the writer's curse. You either write or make yourself and everyone near you miserable because you are not writing. But writers also need to be doing other things if they are going to have anything interesting to say.

I am also a leader—have been since the fifth grade. So I need to lead. And to lead in person. Writing can be a form of leadership, but it's not the same as an actual team effort. I love teamwork. I get thoroughly jazzed working with a group of intelligent, energized people to solve a problem. My community is beginning to discover this, so I need to be careful. Saying yes to every leadership opportunity offered me might become overwhelming. Saying yes to the right ones gives me synchronicity. Things happen because of these roles that bring other opportunities I need into my life. Which ones are the right ones? The ones that feel right in my gut.

My family situation is stable and easy. My two sons are grown with families of their own, and both live near me. This is more of a surprise than you would think. I live near Tacoma, Washington. My boys also live in the Pacific Northwest, even though one was born in Kellogg, Idaho and the other in Claremont, New Hampshire. They spent their early years in Omaha and their high school years in Colorado Springs. College was in Missouri and Colorado respectively. I count my blessings that they are so close.

At one point, I assumed this meant they were supposed to be a big part of my life and that they were *supposed* to include me in theirs extensively. They're not and they don't and that's far more realistic. They have their own lives, social circles, and work challenges. They don't have time to sneeze. I'm healthy, happy, and quite capable of entertaining myself. So we don't get together all that often.

Occasionally I toy with the idea of living somewhere else. When I get down on this area for being "way out on the edge of the country," and think about moving to say… Sedona, I tell myself I'd probably get as much time with my kids if I flew in for a three-day visit several times a year. And that is probably accurate. But I like it here, and I am glad they are here.

My *brothers* are a different story. We all grew up in Wisconsin and the other four siblings are still back there. But somehow two of my brothers and I all ended up in the Puget Sound region. This has been far more fun than I ever expected. Much as our childhoods were filled with family activities and fun, we have all been pretty independent as adults. With three of us together out here, we seem to have reverted to some of the best elements of our shared childhood. We like to play together—like little kids in the basement. One year we built my Christmas tree. (You read that correctly.) And we like to help each other. There are often periods or seasons where I see more of my brothers than my sons. I finally understand this is exactly as it should be.

Socially, I am having a blast, but it is a recent effort that makes it this way. I will not bore you with the list of memberships, but it suffices to say I like to get into things. I enjoy the people I spend time with. But I am also very happy alone. In fact, if there are too many nights of meetings and social fun in a row, I start to get restless. Time home alone in the evening is very rejuvenating for me, especially making myself a nice dinner and eating it with a proper table setting, music, and wine. I am currently single and am fine with that. But I know myself well enough to expect that I am likely to couple again eventually.

I flunked shopping a long time ago and no matter how many times I retake the course, I flunk again. I am just not that interested in spending time to spend money. I have begun to acquire gear for the things I like to do though. Some of that is expensive, but I'm pacing myself so that I don't spend for all of it at once. Last year, the downhill skis and boots. This year, a good road bike. Next year, the kayak.

I've been a saver and a budgeter since my first paying job when I was seven, so money is not one of the major challenges for me. That said, I still need to get back to making money because money is one way to keep score in terms of the complexity of the work you do. And I need complexity. Lots of it. In many forms. If it doesn't come with work, I will make it in projects I undertake at home. I could write a book—and a funny one at that—about how to complicate a project. And about how to do it in the name of not spending money,

The situation with my health is dumbfounding. This is the best health I have *ever* experienced. I can hike 10 miles in a day—sometimes with a couple thousand feet of elevation gain—and come home and mow the lawn. I love to downhill ski and bike. If I overdo it, I might have to ice my knees—but that's true for my 33-year-old son, too. The only thing I'm thinking maybe I should not do is play volleyball. I haven't decided yet.

When I played in my 30s, my competitive instincts left little room to be careful with my body. If I do the same dumb things now, I might miss more important fun because of an injury.

My personality requires LOTS of complexity and variety. If you want to make me miserable, ask me to do the same thing again and again. I look for the lessons in everything I do and need new things to learn to feel alive. I need to be part of a team. It's not essential that I lead it, but that happens quite a bit. I love to be physically active and will incorporate that in my lifestyle from here on. It would be as hard to give that up as breathing.

I've done a lot to define myself spiritually. I'll get into that more later, but I want to acknowledge my belief that everything happens the way it's supposed to. Even the sad, bad, and ugly stuff has lessons. I want to learn them, partly because I love to learn but also because I don't want to have to live through them again because I didn't get it the first time.

The outrage I feel about how life between 60 and 85 is assumed to be marginal energizes me now. That cause isn't likely to sustain me for the rest of my life though. That would be okay. Great in fact. We need those changes as a nation NOW. Besides, I change damn near everything every seven years or so. The Silver Rebellion is certainly my fire at the moment. Each of us came to do something. None of us was designed to be superfluous or to become obsolete. We all have our own special work to do. I like that.

And it's work that feels like play that we're going to do now. I like that even more.

Chapter Four:

Nuts and Bolts and Other Physical Stuff

Last weekend I had the chance to attend a party at a friend's house on the water. This particular friend is a decidedly free spirit. By the time I got to the party, it had moved down the street. The big reason for the change of venue was the presence of three preschoolers. The new location had a fence between the kids and the Sound. It also had room for a kiddie pool inside the fence.

One of the kids was a brown-eyed, two-year-old cutie named Alexander. He was the only grandson of one of the guests and a great lesson for all of us. Alexander liked to be naked. His grandma had regaled us with stories about this at some point prior, but it was still really fun to watch.

Grandma put his swimsuit on, and he went to splash in the pool. Soon, the suit was off, and the kid was *au naturel*. He spent the afternoon that way, in and out of the water. Occasionally an adult would "help" him and put the suit back on. Alexander didn't fuss or fight. He just took the trunks off again as soon as he had the chance.

He knew what he liked and what he wanted and was not afraid to claim it.

Somewhere between age two and retirement, we lose that knack. We let what we want get buried under tons of other information. Our responsibility to take care of ourselves falls prey to our sense of duty to others. We let other people we care about have the final say on "what we want." As a result, on the brink of retirement, it's common to have no idea of what truly appeals to you. Common, but horribly disconcerting. Even the concept of needing *anything* is hard for some of us.

As we start to remedy this, the first place to look is at the physical world. Claiming the colors you enjoy or your favorite kind of music are reasonably easy steps back into that time when we could have gone naked without a world-crushing load of guilt. To know what you like, need, and want to pursue, you need to know YOU...physically, mentally, emotionally, and spiritually.

This chapter looks at the physical part—first at the situation with your physical self, then at aspects of the physical environment you currently inhabit and whether this is the situation you want to continue for your retirement.

Over My Not Quite Dead Body

Okay, let's talk about bodies. Bodies that have been around a while. What kind of equipment are you driving on the road of life? A vintage performance car or a coaster bike with bad brakes? Are you excusing the dents, dings, rust, and accumulated bird poop with "I'm old. What can you expect?"

A helluva lot more than that.

There is no reason to accept an old clunker of a body at this point in your life. But this is, of course, where the parallel between cars and bodies starts to diverge. You can buy a new car. You're looking at using your body another 40 years. The only option you have if it's not in good condition now is to restore it. But that's not so bad. Think about it. Which is cooler, a new Mustang convertible that anyone with the money can acquire or one from 1965 in cherry condition? Vintage has character. Now clean the damn thing up and get it running as well as it can.

Some of you are saying, "Well, she's not talking to ME. I have _____ (you fill in the blank) and that means my days of physical health are over." Not true. I'm talking to you along with everyone else. You may have the disease, disability, or whatever, but you still have the option of making yourself as physically strong as possible. Remember Christopher Reeve?

I'm not suggesting we all need to be able to climb mountains, run marathons, and trek Nepal at this stage. I'm just not going to let you get away with claiming "age" or illness as a reason to not do what you can. When you take the easy way and let yourself be "unable," you deny yourself an incredible amount of the good life. If you're focused on what you can't do, getting through each day becomes a matter of enduring the same thing, over and over. When you focus on what you *can* do, *want* to do, and *are preparing* to do, it's an adventure. Life is vastly sweeter when *lived* than when endured.

When you accept infirmity rather than working toward your own best health, you also put an extra burden on the people who love you. Sure, it's nice to feel the love of "being taken care of." But the price is pretty steep. Dependency is a hard road in any form. People have their own lives to live. Doing all you can for yourself will go a long way toward maintaining good relationships with your family and friends.

Even more important, when you simply accept you "can't" because of a physical condition, you remove yourself from a great deal of the fun you could still be having. Don't assume you can't do it because "people with my condition can't do that." Test your own boundaries. Be creative in how you deal with your limits. It's your choice all over again. Do you want to spend your life and money focused on downing pills and reading magazines in waiting rooms? Why not find out what kind of fun you can have anyway?

The fitness and health area is probably the largest reservoir of conflicting information we will ever create on this Earth. If you look hard enough, you can find a study that will support pretty much any choice you want to make. Peanut butter diet? Sure. Eggs as good nutrition? Yep. Eggs as death by cholesterol. Of course. Running as bad for you? Seen it.

You can find support for what you want to do—or not do, sure. But that doesn't mean it's the truth your body deserves. Because, guess what? This is an area where your instincts are going to tell you what's right for YOU. Your body doesn't need all of what thousands of researchers clamor to have you adopt. Your body needs to be listened to. That's the best way to know what it really needs.

We all need certain basic things. Any body needs to be fed properly. It needs to be maintained. And it needs to be used wisely—with the same care you'd use any piece of important equipment. But these needs are unique to you in how they are accomplished and it's up to you to figure out your own maintenance and fuel requirements.

Fuel….nutrition. Okay, how about nutrition? I'm not going to bore you with the food pyramid. I will not advise you to throw out all the junk food (although I am sorely tempted). All I want you to grasp here—in case you haven't already—is that your body will tell you what it needs. But you have to learn to listen.

For example, what I used to interpret as "hunger pangs" usually means I'm short on water. So I drink a glass or two of water before I start looking for food. I've learned I get in a funk if I eat a lot of refined sugar, particularly if I am not getting much sunshine at the time. I've learned that if I don't eat some good fat at lunchtime, I will be too hungry before dinner—and will resort to junk as a quick solution. For my body, the food guidelines are "produce and protein." For yours, it may be vegan choices. Please don't take my word for it though. Pay attention to what your body does best with.

How do you discover this kind of stuff? It usually starts with external sources of information—a class or a book. But once you have the basic knowledge, it's a case of paying attention to what your body tells you—just like noticing when your car doesn't like the brand or grade of gas you gave it.

My mom was an advocate of wise eating habits back when Wonder Bread was still being touted as nutritional genius. I knew about vitamin C and orange juice in second grade. But it doesn't take the kind of mothering I had to grasp the important things. If you take in more calories than you burn, you gain weight. If you use more calories than you take in, you lose weight. Eating food that still looks like what it started as will keep your nutrients higher and your additives lower. Corn on the cob rather than corn chips. A steak instead of prepared frozen pot roast. An orange—not that orange flavored Popsicle.

I eat red meat. My body needs it. I don't eat dried beans—they don't work for me. Ice cream? Yes, but I have little dish, not the entire carton. It's my own scheme, and it works. I'm in great health, at the right weight, and have more energy than I did in my 20's. I got there by learning to listen to my body instead of food ads and infomercials.

There are two things it's best to always refuse to eat (along with eggplant and squid)—no matter what kind of body you have. They are "should" and "shouldn't." They never taste good, no matter who offers them. And they usually result in weight gain. (Guilt or a sense of failure are so easily soothed with something sweet, fat-laden, and nutritionally barren.) Feed yourself with respect. Feed yourself with appreciation. Feed yourself with the expectation that you are going to be using this body for a good long time. Lay off the guilt.

If you want retirement to be fun, you need to take care of yourself physically. What you eat is the obvious first step in that. Grabbing a fast food "meal" at the drive through and gulping it down as you rush between work and a meeting is an insult to your body, to whatever gave itself to be your food, and to the force of life that includes you. You can do better than that. How is up to you.

Another area you need to look at in terms of your physical well-being is, of course, exercise. Should and shouldn't are just as useless here. Do it because you like to do it. Find something you *do* like to do. Or find something you want to do that you need to get in shape to be able to accomplish. But please, don't exercise "because it's good for me." I have always been in awe of people who run every day and hate it. That seems like such a waste of a good time that could be had doing something else that was physically active and a lot more fun.

Geneen Roth was even more straightforward about the situation in her column for *Prevention* magazine. "The whole idea that we've taken our basic, joyful impulse to move our bodies and reduced it to the drudgery of 30-minutes-three-times-a-week exercise is crazy-making and guilt producing." We've replaced the delight of being outdoors with grin-and-bear-it routines on a bunch of machines in sterile indoor spaces. Now why are we willing to settle for that?

The best way to be physically fit at any age is to know the things you like to do that require physical activity and find ways to do them. You can develop your upper body strength in the garden—or kayaking. Leg muscles and endurance can come on the trail. Core strength might be part of a yoga practice or transformative dancing. Since I like to do so many active things, I also do stretching and free weights on a regular basis. These are not because "I want to be physically fit." They are so that I can bike, hike, ski, skate, dance, play volleyball, and do whatever else I decide I want to do when I get the chance. This is the way it worked when we were kids. It takes so much of the thinking and guesswork out of it. Do what you need to do to get your body in good enough shape to do what you enjoy.

And then don't stop! It's not enough to train so you can do one six-mile hike in July. Hike every week if you like to hike. And if you can't find anything you like to do, invent it. Years ago, my brother and his wife came up with their own version of "golf", using Frisbees, because it helped them be active. They would work their way through various local parks, designating things as "holes" as they covered the route. There was a lot of laughter as they tried to get their discs where they intended—and a lot of steps to retrieve them when they went off course. Disc golf has developed since they started their game. Now they play on actual disc golf courses. But then they didn't know they existed and would not have had all that physical fun without some ingenuity.

Books on fitness and nutrition proliferate faster than rabbits. If this is an area where you need some outside guidance before you begin to rely on your own radar, then browse the bookstore or the library shelves. What you need will be there. But once you understand the basics, listen to your body for further instruction. That's where the most useful truth resides. However, if your body is telling you to eat three jelly donuts and take a nap instead of walking in the sunshine for an hour, retune the dial. You're listening to interference.

THE ENERGY FACTOR

Losing weight probably gets more attention than even how to make money in terms of number of published pages. Gaining energy is probably a better focus for good health. The attention given to that is almost nil. Jim Loehr and Tony Schwartz provide a convincing and practical framework for managing your existing energy—instead of your time—in *The Power of Full Engagement*. It's great information and strategy, but there's more to it than that. We need the battle cry of the old Frito Lay commercial… "We'll make more."

People in traditional retirement can be pretty subdued. Is this because they don't have the energy to do things or because they don't know what to do? It's my firm belief that the first thing we need to do to move to a better version of retirement is admit how boring the current version can be.

The effect of the existing stereotype—that when people retire, they are worn out and run down—is subtle. If you do admit you need more, your friends and family are likely to laugh—or tell you how much they envy your chance to do nothing. You begin to think there's something wrong with you because you "want more." This "right" to do nothing is the source of other's envy, after all. It's embarrassing to admit you don't know how to be happy with it.

A side effect of this is that our society functions as if "nothing" is all those who have retired are *capable* of. The assumption, in terms of employers in particular, is that once we leave, we are finished—beyond any possible usefulness to get the work done. That's not it at all. *Not having* to go to work is a whole different set of issues than *not being able* to go to work. There might be a smidgen of truth to the "unable" assumption for specific employees—those with health issues that precipitated retirement, for example. But for most people who elect to retire these days, the idea that they become instantly incompetent is ridiculous.

Who started this idea that at 65 you need to retire?

You're not going to believe this. Ken Dychtwald, a guru on the social aspects of aging, explains in his book *Age Power* that this marker for "old age" was first proposed for *German* workers by Otto van Bismark in *1881*. Germans who reached age 65 in 1881 really were old. The life expectancy was less than that. When the United States initiated Social Security in 1935, life expectancy of the average American was still only 63. It is now closing in on 80. Even more amazing, every modernized nation in the world took 65 as its standard threshold of "old age" for its government programs, except for the few who set it at 60. They are all still using the same markers! This is lunacy.

The 60 to 85 age frame offers huge opportunity to *increase* energy levels. We have more time to be physically active—which increases energy. We are better able to focus on eating well as we take the time for it—which improves energy. We have less stress—an energy bandit if there ever was one. And we are more prone to look into spirituality at this stage of our lives—an energy booster with huge potential. So for starters, please stop assuming you will not have the energy to do that thing you've always dreamed of doing. See what you can do to "make more" before you give up the idea of doing what excites you.

There's another aspect of energy we need to look at. It helps a lot to be aware of your *current* energy level. Or, more accurately, your natural energy level. I found this out the hard way. I need a lot going on. A hard life for me is one that lacks stimulation, variety, and lots of activity. Yet when I walked into my life as a writer, I assumed I needed to make writing my sole focus and to stay at it for at least eight hours every day. Sit butt in chair and stay there.

This is just plain not me. Trying to do it that way made it impossible for me to do it at all. I'm finding now that wedging my writing in between other commitments actually results in a more productive effort than staring at the screen all day long. Know your own natural pace and work style and honor it.

It's also important to recognize the difference between the rate you like to operate at and that of the significant others in your life. If you are a cougar, walking with a turtle all day is going to get to you. Likewise if you are an armadillo and live with a gazelle. But meeting for dinner and talking about your separate adventures might be really fun. No one can define the right solution for you on this kind of stuff, but you have to. Taking the time to acknowledge these differences and plan for them can go a long way toward keeping your relationship vibrant and you happily coupled.

NEW STUFF

Learning new things should be a big part of this stage in life. Areas of improvement are not limited to bridge and golf either. The mental aspects will get more attention in the next chapter. But from the get-go, let's get one thing straight. *We can still learn*—to watercolor, to draw blood as a nursing student, to windsurf. The things we choose to learn need to be true aspects of ourselves though. When we get this far, we tend to lose interest if it's not part of the Real Me. There's nothing to MAKE you do it if it doesn't really interest you. You won't get fired. You won't have to take the kids out of school to move. What looks like an inability could be just a lack of desire. That's another argument for knowing as much as you can about yourself.

This year, I went back to downhill skiing after being away from it for 10 years. I was a mediocre skier at best when I lived in Colorado. I went then because it was something I was "supposed" to like. I did like it, but I was too wound up in my fears to be able to enjoy it. I've eliminated much of the fear and respect the rest a lot more now. I am having huge fun learning to ski again—and am already skiing better than I ever did in my younger years.

There's another realm of new stuff that warrants some discussion here—the mind-body connection and alternative medicine. There are many names for it: energy medicine, alternative medicine, alternative therapies. This one may elicit some fear—or derision—if you haven't been near the topic. Don't push it away so fast. Sometimes, it's exactly what you need even if you weren't looking for it.

This stuff often doesn't follow the scientific method or a rational model. There are organizations like the Institute of Noetic Sciences who are trying to build better bridges in that regard. They support research in this arena that comes closer to the rigor of standard physical science. But for the most part, this stuff is just "out there" and you find it under duress. Often, it comes into play when the usual solutions aren't working.

And sometimes by total accident. Personally, I would have never started with it intentionally. I grew up having to "state my source" for points I was trying to make in dinner conversation. My college degrees are in disciplines that require scientific rigor. Everything had to be grounded in someone else's research. I thought I was calling a traditional psychotherapist to talk about why I wanted to move to the Pacific Northwest when I contacted an energy practitioner early in my exploration of that step. She was just what I needed to get to the pith of the situation quickly. Talk about an express ride to insight.

There's an entire section on the mind/body connection and related topics at most general interest bookstores. If you haven't gotten a personal nudge to explore it, you probably think it's for people who wear weird clothes and name their dogs with Tibetan words. Some of it, by authors like Larry Dossey, Bernie Siegel, and Deepak Chopra has credibility because of their credentials as medical doctors. But it's more than just a rebellion from the traditional Western version of medicine. It considers health, wellness, and illness on a whole different plane.

Unless these few words make you want to find these authors, you probably don't need to explore it right now. Just remember to keep an open mind when you are looking for physical or mental health solutions. If someone suggests something in this arena, check it out with more than your mind. Trust your gut—not your ability to do good scientific research—on whether you should explore in one of these areas. Trust your intuition, not your girlfriend, spouse, hunting buddy, or family physician. Sometimes this area contains sources of incredible insight and awesome breakthroughs not to mention outright mental or physical healing. But as with all things involving humans, some of what is offered are scams. You're gonna have to be the judge. Your intuitive sense of the worth of what you're considering is the most accurate source of information you'll have for evaluating stuff like this.

Putting It in Context

Getting your body to perform as you want is only half of what you need to consider in the physical realm. You also need to take a good look at your physical environment in terms of what you want. Where does this physical YOU exist now? How is that working?

PLACE

Articles on "the best places to retire" come out with the same regularity as they used to on "best colleges at which to party." *Fortune* magazine recently decided Boulder, Colorado; Kiawah Island, South Carolina; Sarasota, Florida; Athens, Georgia, and Maui, Hawaii were "where to retire in style." They considered the population, the average daily temperature, and highlights of the area—such as "great food," "tax breaks," and "highly rated golf courses" in reaching their decisions. In case you want to give them the benefit of the doubt, the lead-in to the article was "We get it: You are consumed with golf. Or fly-fishing. Or you dream of living where the surf is up—but the taxes aren't." Do not use this kind of crap to make your decisions. No, *Fortune*, you do NOT get it.

Choosing where to live based on these kinds of shallow considerations will have you either moving again and again or miserable. There is no place that has a *perfect* climate. No matter where you live, there will be things you don't like about the area. Your choices will be more solid—and leave you far more satisfied—if you make them from a well of information that goes deeper than the number of golf courses within 30 miles.

Perhaps you are already living in the ideal physical environment. Maybe you are and don't realize it. Are you close enough to the kids, but not too close? Are there things about the weather you like most of the time? In terms of geographic location, can you do what makes your heart sing where you live now? If golf is what you want to do, then golf courses are relevant. If you think playing once or twice a week is enough, there are other things you will be using more of your time for. Use *those* things to decide where to live.

Do you like the place you call home? Can you maintain it without resenting that you own it? This goes for more than the house, condo, or apartment, incidentally. If you've been a good soldier in the Consumer Army, you have "stuff" that takes a lot of your time and money to care for as well.

STUFF

For many of us, this time of our lives involves streamlining. We give family things to our kids. We give clothing to the local mission. We give whatever we can to whomever we see who can use it. We finally grasp that the stuff is not as important as the simplicity not having it allows.

The best part of this need to streamline is finding really cool places that need your stuff. When I decided to divest of a third of my books (hundreds) a couple years ago, I contacted a used bookstore. The owner made me aware of a local effort to collect "stock" for a veteran returning from the Persian Gulf so he could restart his used bookstore. I got to help someone who deserved all the help he could get. Cool.

TIME

How about the way you use your time? Are you happy with that? What's most difficult for you when you don't have enough time for everything you want to do? What's hardest about having *more* time than you need to get what's on the agenda accomplished? Time is a human construct. We make it. And then, too often, we let it define our lives without much effort to put it where we want it. *What do you want to do with your time?*

WORK STRUCTURE

If you're considering "work" as part of your plan, what kind of commitment would serve you best? Most of us have been working "regular jobs" that demand presence and performance at prescribed times every day every week. There are many other ways to structure work. Would some other format give you the kind of flexibility you want?

A contract with a project orientation can give you an intense sense of focus and involvement and still leave you with the freedom to do whatever you want between projects. You could also become an expert resource—called in only when that specific expertise is needed. I have a ski friend who does this. He's an internationally well-regarded engineer who specializes in marine turbines. He goes all over the world to head up projects to keep the engines on big ships running properly. But not when he wants to ski.

Another option is the piecework approach. You commit to getting a certain amount of work done within a certain timeframe rather than committing time-on-the-job specifically. Job sharing is likely to become more popular as retiring boomer skills become more essential, too. This could even be a team effort between three or four similarly competent people so the job is covered fulltime but who's doing it at any given moment is elastic.

It's your call. You might find working the first three days of the first three weeks of every month the perfect way to pursue your other interests while still keeping your hand in things. You won't know what works until you know what you want to do though. So we are back to the same advice yet again. Figure out what you want.

As you do this part of your planning, be sure to consider *all* your relevant assets. I'm not talking about mutual funds and a savings account here. This is about the intangible stuff. What *could* you do to make money if you needed to? What could you do on a barter basis if it got you what you needed? I count my skills as a writer—many different ways—when I look at this. But I also count my experience as a project manager, planner, cook, seamstress, outdoor enthusiast, and gardener. My older son would include the fact that he can weld and is SCUBA certified. If he didn't want to work as a groundwater geologist, he could make a good living as an underwater welder. (Right. He is pretty amazing.)

The physical decisions around work relate to "where" you work along with "when." Do you want to be able to take your job south for the winter? Home Depot has a program where some of its associates do just that. Do you want to go to an office? Do you want to travel as part of your work? Or would you rather work at home? In the garage? At the computer? In the kitchen? Possibilities abound. Close you eyes and think about the physical site where you would have the most fun working.

Any surprises?

PLAY

Now let's think about play. Yes, that is part—an important part—of well-lived retirement. How do you like to play? What are your favorite things to do as fun? Are they the things you've been doing? Sometimes, what you like to do took too much time so you substituted something else. For example, playing tennis takes a lot less time than playing golf. If you could be a kid again, what kinds of things would be the most fun to do? If someone *required* you to play for four hours a day, how would you spend the time?

You may need to be somewhere else entirely to do what you like to do for play. If you live in Manhattan and like to hike, your decisions about play will be different than if you live in Boulder, Colorado and like to hike. The manner in which you honor your need for a certain kind of play is up to you. For example, if you're a hiker and live in an area where hiking is mostly walks along alfalfa fields, you could move to a place with better hiking. But you could also continue to live where you do and plan a series of trips to different hiking locations, take a temporary job in a area with good hiking every once in a while, or become a guide for the season so that you don't have to change where you live.

HOME

Another aspect of your immediate environment is "home." Where you live is going to be more important if you're going to be there all the time. Do you like your current living arrangement? Are there things about this place that you cherish beyond words? Or do you pray for a tornado to flatten it so that you can start over?

Are you authentically reflected in where you're living? Hard as I tried, I couldn't get away from living in "the Lloyd Museum" when I was married. I felt like I was at someone else's home because so much of the furniture and decorative elements were from his family. Are the walls painted colors you like? Do you have places for your stuff specifically? Is what you see when you come home soothing or the source of frustration?

Are you planning to build a new nest? The romance of building your dream home is intoxicating. Take the time to be sure you want that life before you talk to the architect or the log home dealer though. Once you're there, getting back is a lot harder.

Geography Solutions

I've included this as a separate section because it's an area that is particularly fraught with peril in the years just after you stop going to work every day. This is true both because so many of us think we are going to spend all our time traveling and because so many of us think in terms of moving somewhere else to live as soon as we can.

TRAVEL

Nepal. Antarctica. Paris. Black Rock City, Nevada. We all have places we want to go see. Travel is high on most people's lists when they no longer have to show up for work every morning. We want to go and do in all the ways we couldn't when we were job-bound. When we start down this track, we expect we'll travel for the rest of our lives. It usually doesn't work that way.

We were on a trip to Guadalajara when I learned this. Some new friends from Montana were listening to us describe where we'd been that year. "Newly retired, right?" they asked when we finally let them get a word in edgewise. They laughed and told us they'd become a lot more selective after several years and suggested we would, too. They were right—but it took us a couple more years to learn it.

The lures of travel are legion. To see new places, of course. But also to learn new skills—such as a language or a mode of travel (trekking or cycling). And to have great stories to tell when you get home. Watch out for that last one. If you are traveling to impress people, you are on the wrong track.

Traveling to see kids and grandkids is fun—sometimes. Being at their beck and call as a fill-in babysitter is something you want to be very sure about before you agree to it. Once it starts, it's hard to stop. And it's a long time from birth to high school graduation.

Although I have been known to get in the car for a ride around the block, there are two situations where I think travel is a bad idea. Do not go because there is a timeshare available. And do not go to get away from the weather. Trying to get away from the weather is an admission you have nothing more important to worry about.

Letting timeshare availability decide what you are going to do with your life makes about as much sense as letting the neighbors arrange your garage to meet their needs. Do what you want to do if you are going to travel. Anything less is a waste of time, money, and energy.

CHANGING PLACES

The second geography solution is a bit more extreme—moving to a new location when you retire. This is the dream scenario. Retire. Move somewhere warm…and sunny…and new. Be careful with this one in particular. Starting over is just that. You begin again with everything from where to buy your groceries to who to trust with your hair, your bank account, and your cardiac problem.

To be sure, it is, sometimes, the right call. But think about all the ins and outs when you consider it. If you choose to live somewhere different when you leave work, you are giving up even more of the network you have established. You are giving up the familiarity that makes the everyday things easy. But you are also giving up your favorite ruts. It's your call. Just make it from a well-informed position. Know what you are leaving behind and whether you are going to wish you hadn't.

There are ways to give "the new geography" solution a test spin. When I wanted to move to the Seattle area, my spouse was convinced "I" would not like it. (He'd lived here while he was in the Navy. *He* had not liked it.) I suggested a three-month trial during the winter—which I dubbed the Drizzle Tolerance Test. We spent January through March in the Pacific Northwest in a furnished apartment near the kids who'd just provided us with a new grandson.

Yes, there were more gray days than in Colorado. And there was rain. But you don't have to shovel rain. My spouse played golf—a lot. I learned what gardening at sea level would be like. It was an El Nino year—the weather was much better than usual. So of course we moved. Even with a less than complete picture of just how wet things get during "gray season" in the Pacific Northwest, we knew a lot more about what we were getting into than if we'd have just come out and started looking for real estate. (I have to add though, that the next winter was one of the wettest on record. By the middle of November we were looking for plans for an ark.)

HYBRIDS AND PROTOTYPES

Perhaps a better strategy for adding excitement to your geography is temporary things that take anywhere from several months to several years at different locations. Doing a stint in the Peace Corps in Morocco, for example. Or backpacking across Europe. The opportunities to do helping things in exotic—or at least remote and unusual—places are already available with outfits like Earthwatch Institute on a short-term basis. Options for this kind of experience will only increase as the baby boom starts to want them. These kinds of assignments have an added benefit. No matter where you live, when you get back to your own digs, you feel like you are living in a palace.

Another version of this is to do disaster relief. Those assignments are usually of a shorter duration than something like the Peace Corps, but longer than a "helping vacation." I strongly recommend you not do them as a way to travel. There's a lot more to disaster relief than "travel." When you hit the scene, the geography is typically in pretty bad shape. Doing disaster relief work is demanding emotionally. We'll look at volunteerism further under emotional considerations. But let's be very clear about this point right now: Going to help with a disaster as a way to see that part of the country or the world is a very bad idea for all concerned.

THE SKY IS THE LIMIT

Your options are limitless in terms of what you might find fulfilling regarding your physical situation in retirement. To make any sense of it so you can create a plan for achieving it, you have to start by acknowledging what is important to you now in where you live, how you live, and what's a part of it. If the thought of not being able to hug your grandchildren every few days throws you into a panic, moving to Florida while they remain in Michigan is not going to fetch it. But if you've been anticipating a move to a warmer climate for years, have identified a location, have vacationed there numerous times, and already have friends and resources established there, such a move makes more sense.

I'm not suggesting you have to stay where you are if you haven't done anything to prepare to live elsewhere. I am insisting that it's going to take a more extensive effort to be sure you set yourself up to succeed in the new environment.

Stories abound about people who moved to retirement meccas and then either moved again or moved back home after a couple years. Know what you are getting into, what you are leaving, what you need in your life to make it work, and how you are going to get that at the new location. If you do it, for heavens sake, do it right.

One last thought on this subject: Mates. This is a decidedly difficult area to maneuver if the two of you don't want the same thing. In that instance, temporary solutions might help flesh out a workable long-term approach. Also individual temporary solutions might make sense from time to time. You go to New York City where it's so easy for you to re-charge and she can go tag big horn sheep with the wildlife people in the Colorado Rockies for a week or two.

Think and Do

Every time we get this far, I hope you do the exercises. They are fun. They will help you develop a large knowledge base about yourself relatively painlessly. I'm not going to pussyfoot around any more. DO THE DAMN EXERCISES. They are here as a way for you to tap information you need to make solid decisions. The effort just might save you from wandering around in circles for 13 years.

Exercise 4.1 — LET'S GET PHYSICAL

A multiple choice test—sort of. You can choose more than one, but the real meat will be in what you write after each section.

NUTRITION

1. **For me, the most perfect food combination is:**

    a.) meat and potatoes

    b.) red wine and chocolate

    c.) soup and salad

    d.) cereal and milk

    e.) whatever is in the refrigerator

2. **When it comes to my efforts at nutrition, I'm like:**

    a.) Woody Allen (neurotic)

    b.) John Wayne (in denial)

    c.) Tom Hanks (sensitive and caring)

    d.) Arnold Schwarzenegger (in charge)

    e.) Mr. Magoo (confused)

3. **My current nutritional habits are:**

    a.) ugly

    b.) well-intended but short on follow through

    c.) pretty well focused

    d.) my mother's worst nightmare

    e.) my spouse's job

If I want to keep my body working as well as it can, my commitment to feeding myself authentically needs to include:

_____

_____

_____

PHYSICAL ACTIVITY

4. **I most enjoy exercise when:**

   a.) I am watching someone else do it.

   b.) I'm sure my heart's beating at the target rate and I'm doing it right.

   c.) I get it unintentionally.

   d.) I can beat someone at something while doing it.

   e.) I can get away by myself to do it.

5. **My idea of a long walk is:**

   a.) a drive in the national forest with a two-mile walk on a self-guided nature trail.

   b.) going to the mailbox.

   c.) hiking the entire Pacific Crest Trail.

   d.) three hours at the mall.

   e.) playing 18 holes of golf.

6. **I intend to keep myself physically fit once I leave work by:**

   a.) claiming total control of the TV remote and clicking it constantly.

   b.) walking with my spouse, friends, or pet.

   c.) taking up the sport of _____.

   d.) playing with my grandkids.

   e.) working on the house and yard.

What concerns me most about staying physically fit and healthy after I leave work is:

_____

_____

_____

ENERGY

7. **On a typical day, I have about as much energy as:**

   a.) road kill.

   b.) my grandkid's teddy bear.

   c.) a hydroelectric plant.

   d.) a meteor.

   e.) the last losing sports team I rooted for.

8. **My most extreme couch potato (low energy) behavior is:**

   a.) spending an hour on the phone with a friend.

   b.) sleeping for 10 hours straight when I am healthy.

   c.) taking a three-hour nap with the TV on.

   d.) spending the entire weekend watching football on television.

   e.) none of the above. Other:_____

9. **To boost my energy I typically:**

   a.) meditate or pray.

   b.) drink another cup of coffee.

   c.) go for a walk.

   d.) eat some healthy source of calories like an energy bar.

   e.) take time to breathe.

After I stop working, I want enough energy that I can:

_____

_____

_____

To do what I want to be able to do for the rest of my life, my body needs:

_____

_____

_____

Exercise 4.2—NEST FEATHERS

Write down your first thought—smart retorts included.

The most important thing about where I live: _____

_____

_____

The thing that bugs me about where I live: _____

_____

_____

The balance between what I like and don't like about where I live right now is:

_____

_____

The place I would live instead if I could figure out how: _____

_____

_____

If I won the lottery, the place I live would: _____

_____

_____

What do you like about where you live? What do you dislike? What would you solve by moving somewhere else? What do you think you would miss?

Where you live and how long you are willing to stay in the same place is uniquely personal. I come from a family where people count the years in their homes in decades. I am not able to do that. The longest I've lived anywhere as an adult was fifteen years and that was a lot longer than I wanted. Take the time to figure out your own preferences on this. Once you sell the house, you are somewhere else, whether it's really for you or not.

Exercise 4.3—TRAVEL BUGS

List the 10 places you would like to see the most.

1._____

2._____

3._____

4._____

5._____

6._____

7._____

8._____

9._____

10._____

Now add how long you would spend at each place and why you want to go see it. _____

_____

_____

If you don't have 10 places you would like to go see, list the reason why doing that doesn't appeal to you: _____

_____

_____

Seeing what other parts of the country and the world are like is a form of education. Many of us yearn for the opportunity to go see what's "out there." But if you like home perfectly well and have no need to go wandering, be honest and admit it. A couple who meets disparate needs honestly will fare far better than the duet who insists on going together even though one of them is miserable being away from home. This goes for friends as well as spouses and kids.

Exercise 4.4—TEMPORARY GEOGRAPHY

Under what circumstances would the following options appeal?

Doing a two-year stint with the Peace Corps:

_____

_____

_____

Temporarily trading homes with someone who lives in a different country:

_____

_____

_____

Backpacking in a foreign country:

_____

_____

_____

Taking employment in a foreign country:

_____

_____

_____

Do any of the above options make your heart beat a bit faster? If any of them appeal, what makes them seem like fun? Are there other ways that offer the same kind of fun? Is there a temporary change of geography you might want to pursue?

For me to do a temporary change of geography:

_____

_____

_____

This may not be something you are interested in at all. But thinking about it may trigger something that is. Have some fun. Play with this. Example: "I would only entertain the idea of living in a foreign country if the King of Monaco asked me to train the croupiers at their casinos for six months for a hefty fee with all-expenses paid."

Exercise 4.5—INTANGIBLE ASSETS:

You can do a lot more than what you do/did for a paycheck. List the skills have you developed along the way that you don't use for work, but could.

_____

_____

_____

Here are some from my list: cook, gardener, chocolatier, seamstress, copywriter, paid scribe (love letters, business letters, etc.), practical joke arranger, custom quilt designer, hiking guide, travel writer. If you can't come up with anything, ask your friends and family. They'll have ideas. You may be the ideal candidate for a job tasting junk food. Or testing remote control prototypes for home electronics. Or reading to children at the local hospital.

It's important to flesh out this list. When the source of competence that's paid the bills for so long ceases to be part of your life, it helps to know all the other things you could do if you needed to. And there may be one or two you really want to use.

BARBIE DIES!

Whenever I get the chance, I kill Barbie. That doll should have never been born. Lately, it's been with a hammer when one of my women friends turns 60. (Do you have any idea how indestructible they make that doll?) It should happen a lot sooner. Those of us born female live our entire adult lives in her shadow. Guys aren't any luckier. They get a collage of Gordon Gecko, Superman, and Dennis Rodman as society's set of expectations. Stereotypes all, but a strong silent message about the way our culture *expects* us to behave.

Stereotypes are those lovely oversimplified opinions of how an entire class or age group behaves. What they need. How they think. How they fit into society as a whole. They are all wrong, of course. Aunt Bea is a stereotype—she deserves the hammer, too. As does June Cleaver, Ward Cleaver, and Betty Crocker. The truth about each of us is that we are different. Stereotypes deny that truth.

At this point in our lives, we are faced with the cruelest stereotype of all—the version of "old" that comes with achieving the opportunity to retire. "Old" is not a pretty picture—wrinkled, rumpled, slow, stupid, easy to anger, and insistent on our own petty needs. Greedy. In the way. Is that you? Sure as hell isn't me. I give more of myself with more energy now than I ever have. I'm more tolerant, more patient, and more willing to let the other person have his or her way. And I am doing more complex work.

We even do it to ourselves. Given the power, I would outlaw both menopause and Alzheimer's jokes. They're not funny. They just reinforce this set of lies. But we're making progress. I was delighted last week with a phrase in an e-mail from a dear friend in Omaha. Speaking of the kindergarten teacher both my boys were lucky enough to have, she said, "She's become quite an attractive woman in her older years." This teacher was in her 40s when my kids had her 30 years ago. We are not talking about looking good at 35. We are talking about beauty at 70 and beyond. It exists. We need to celebrate it.

This drivel that you're instantly ugly and in need of massive amounts cosmetic surgery and anti-aging therapies the day you hit 60 has got to go. But we're bombarded with that garbage, and it's hard not to believe it after a while. We need to stop this. Guys need to stop worrying about going gray. For me, gray is a plus with a guy. The other day I caught myself doing a 180 to better see a head of lovely gray male hair. I never did that—or do that—for men who are blonde or brunette. I have no idea why I find gray hair so attractive, but I do. Many women say the same thing about baldness.

The idea that we need to look young is dumb. I don't want to look young. I've been around long enough and learned enough that I want people to see my credibility. Young people aren't credible. They haven't been through enough to prove themselves. I want to look *vibrant*. I want to look like an experienced, capable woman who would be interesting to get to know—because I am. What kind of a conversation do you think you could have with that lithe young thing pouting at you from the fashion magazine? Why would you want to even try to talk to someone looking that sullen?

There's a more insidious problem with this age stereotype though. The part about our not knowing anything, not being able to think well, and not being able to do anything that demands any sort of complex thought is just plain lethal. There is *nothing* to support these assumptions. The research Harkness reviewed led her to conclude "There is no decline in intelligence because of age. No research correlates mental decline with healthy aging, nor proves that job performance is worse with age."

This is, however, what we are up against as we explore what we are going to do next. Many of our options are going to be under that very hard shell of ageism. I'm not suggesting we all roll over and play dead—or that we all go take a collective nap. But how we go about getting the kind of things we want in our lives is going to be different. As a 20-something, you could respond to an ad in the paper and have half a chance of getting the job. As a person old enough to retire, your success would likely be zero. Finding the work and other opportunities you want at this stage depends on how well you build a network within your area of interest and how well you can make what you want to do mesh with the specific needs of an organization or person.

This sounds discouraging, but actually it's just the opposite. This work is about doing what we love. We need to get good at finding who needs us to do that. At finding those others who also love the particular work we love or who need that particular thing done. They won't be coming from the stereotype in how they see us, because they will already be past initial impressions and on to that shared passion. These are the people we need to focus on finding, on getting to know.

There is a strong parallel between what we face now as an age issue and what women faced in the workplace in the 1960s, '70s, and '80s. Then, I was a "girl" who liked to do work the "boys" usually did. Fortunately, I arrived on that scene as some enlightened companies were starting to recognize the value of tapping into the brainpower of the entire population instead of just the male half. I got the chance to do some really challenging things because I was lucky with my timing, but also because I was willing to step up and do the work.

The companies I worked for believed in me, even though I was a "girl", because I did what they needed to get done. I did it well. And sometimes "it" could be pretty ugly. Guys who were furious I'd gotten a position they'd applied for came up to me later and admitted that if they'd have known what the job was going to require, they never would have responded to the posting.

So what? Who cares if some chick made it in a guy's world? The reason I bring it up is that my success then bodes well for our success now. The way we "make it" is to do the job well. And not by working 80 hour weeks. As experienced workers, we have an advantage in that we have done it before. We KNOW things. We're on that same brink in terms of companies starting to see a new way to get the work done. If they can tap what we know in ways that give us what we want of retirement, they have an advantage. It's not a slam-dunk because the stereotype still operates for the majority. But more and more, the opportunities are going to be there. Both because effective companies are catching on and because we are learning where to look and how to negotiate what we want. But we have to *know* what we want.

Ah, back to that. What you want. Where do you look for that? You look where your passion turns you. At the very core of everything we do to make this time of life outstanding is the need to honor and operate from our passion—from the authentic sources of our own excitement. Passion is what gets you talking with someone—for an hour—after you already decided it was time to leave the party. Passion is the article that you start to read—and end up being late for a lunch date because of. Passion is when you see something start to open up in your life and you can't let go of it. You stop everything else to learn more.

Passion is the Real You, awake, alive, and ready to make a difference. And you find it by???

Well. Sorry, but…you find it by knowing yourself. The Real You of the Right Now. This is not about what you loved as a kid. That may be a piece of it. But so is all that you've learned and done and experienced between then and now. Passion is your soul in action. It has to start from who you really are.

Find that person and get to know him/her. Well.

Chapter Five:

Mental Monkey Bars

Remember the monkey bars? That "flat ladder across the sky" at the playground? That thing always intimidated me. First, there was the ladder up. Then the reach—waaaayyyy out. And then, when I finally grabbed on and let myself out on it, hanging from the bars felt like my arms were going to pull out of their sockets. Of course there was more to it than what I understood—I had to learn to do all that and *swing* to have fun on it.

Sometimes thinking is like that—complex beyond what you can comprehend. Those are the times when you look at a project and decide quietly, "No way." I had that reaction when I read Robert Ludlum's *The Bourne Identity*. I was in awe of the number of plot threads he wove so effectively. I told myself to stop believing I was going to be a novelist; no way would I ever be able to do that. Then I left the corporate world and started concentrating on learning to write novels. Now I can do that. Probably never be as good at it as Ludlum, but I know what I need to do to get it done.

The best mental challenges are the ones you think are impossible when you first meet them. They give so much more opportunity to develop your mental muscles. But ya gotta wanna. A complex challenge at this point in life is useless if it isn't something that intrigues you. I helped my daughter-in-law design—and then made—her wedding dress. Definitely a complex mental challenge. But I wouldn't have gotten beyond the first fabric shopping expedition if I hadn't been in love with the idea of helping her create this special dress and getting to know her better in the process.

When you don't look for them purposely, mental challenges can come from really dumb origins. After we moved to the Pacific Northwest, I unintentionally invented a game called "Use It Up" to get mental stimulation I didn't realize I needed.

The Use It Up game was a way of saying "I love you" to the other people I cooked for *and* stretching my mind—with half a cup of leftover garbanzo beans. The point of the game was to find something tasty and interesting to make with the rest of a leftover ingredient. Each solution usually resulted in leftover something-else. So my game went on: use the leftover carrots in a cake that also requires dried currants. Then find a use for the rest of the currants. I know, you non-cooks decided I was nuts in the first sentence about this. Pretty silly, I agree. But I needed something the game gave me.

Mental exercise. Each round of Use It Up was a thinking challenge— Find a recipe that used the specific ingredient (which usually meant reading a *lot* of recipes); find the rest of the ingredients; do the math, if needed, to reduce the recipe to where it would serve two rather than an army platoon; then make the dish. I did this for several *years*.

We are born to think. Our minds are one of our most precious assets. It is absolute lunacy to assume we aren't going to use them any more once we can afford to stop going to work everyday. It's much more fitting for us to be *wise elders* than ninnies in a perpetual fog. Wisdom requires thinking. The idea of giving up thinking makes about as much sense as giving up food.

The traditional expectations of retirement are that we will do just that though. No one is waiting for you to solve that problem any more or to get that complex thing done on the job.

You stop working. You *retire*. You get to do nothing. Eventually you get eccentric. Then maybe you lose your mind entirely. It's all part of aging—or so the story goes. The story is wrong.

In a study reported in the *Brain/Mind Bulletin* and cited by Helen Harkness, one researcher noted "Old people become crazy for three reasons: Because they were crazy when they were young, because they have an illness, or because we drive them crazy—and the last reason is more common." One of the most effective ways to drive anyone crazy is to deny them mental stimulation. We are literally boring people to death.

USE IT OR LOSE IT

Why do people buy in on this? I suspect a big motivator is the value we place, as a society, on being able to get to the point of not working. Most people envy those who "get to retire." How could you not want to do something everyone thinks is so terrific? There is a huge gap between how to "not work" well and the fantasy that resides in our societal mind bank. To do it right, you have to keep on thinking. That's not the current communal picture at all.

Right, a few chapters ago, I said "Don't think." And sometimes your gut *is* going to get you to the right answer faster than your brain. But be selective. When you hear an ad on TV that advises "Ask your doctor if Pill XYZ is right for you," ask yourself why you would go looking for another drug to pay for and deal with side effects from. There is no way a TV ad campaign for a prescription drug is geared to your best interest. Your health care practitioner spent *years* learning medicine. Do you really think a 60-second spot just after the weather report is going to give you better treatment? Listen to your body and your doctor. Ignore those ads. They are there to sell pills not keep you healthy.

In terms of brainpower, it really *is* a "use it or lose it" situation. The more you think, the better you can think. Stuff I am working on now is far more complex than what I tackled as a college student—and what I did then was reasonably impressive. I'm not unique on this. I've been thinking for a long time. Why wouldn't I be better at it now than when I was 20? When we practice, we get better at things. It's part of being human.

This drivel about not being able to think as you get older started when we started treating older people AS IF they couldn't think. I'd love to do an experiment where we put 20-year-olds in wheelchairs and sat them in rows in the halls of a retirement home day after day. I'd insist no one pay attention to anything they said. I bet they would exhibit the exact same behaviors we assume are caused by "aging" in as little or less time than the elders who endure it every day of their lives. This idea that you aren't up to thinking because you've had a lot of birthdays is nuts.

There are many enticements to do just that though, some of them extremely well intentioned. We have cars that think for us. They tell us the door isn't closed and remind us we haven't taken the keys out of the ignition. Companies "think for us" by suggesting other products we might like, "given our previous purchases." Spouses, children, and friends can also end up doing us a disservice by handling stuff we need to think through ourselves. Get advice. Get counsel. Get a lot of different opinions. But for God's sake, figure it out yourself whenever you can.

One of the things that eventually killed the fun of travel when I was married was that I was expected to do—and did—all the thinking about where we were trying to get to. He'd drive; I'd navigate. We decided where we were going to go jointly before we set out, but it was up to me to make sure we got to there without getting lost.

I bought in on this. I need a lot of mental stimulation and this was a way to get it. It was all wrong in terms of a strategy though. Sure, he didn't have to worry about it—short of growling at me if I couldn't give him an answer he needed while we were en route. But I took away his need to think by accepting the task solo. We didn't have a team doing the problem solving. We had an autocracy. He asked and I had to have the answer. Instantly. Doesn't sound like much fun, right? It wasn't.

Worse, I started getting "dumb cow" looks from him when I asked him ordinary things in our ordinary environment. It was too much mental strain for him to decide whether he'd already watered the front garden. I started to panic, thinking his mind was going. It wasn't. But I'd sure helped him put it in the far corner of the guest bedroom closet for a few years. That was wrong of me. If you are thinking for someone else who's capable of thinking (not diagnosed with a physiological disorder), it's also wrong of you.

The reverse is also true. If you hang out with a bunch of people who consider thinking un-American, you're going to lose a lot of what you have to work with because you're embarrassed to use it. If you go to bingo—or Bunco—three nights a week and watch sitcom reruns on the tube the other four, your brain is in mothballs. Your friends are you mental workout buddies. Pay attention to who's actually going to go to the gym. Or, as George Carlin puts it "An idle mind is the devil's playground. And the devil's name is Alzheimer's."

Studies Harkness reviewed concluded, "There is no reason to expect the brain to deteriorate with age, even though many of us are living longer." Try new things. Learn new skills. Look for new areas of interest. Keep up with what's going on in the world. It's as dumb to stop thinking as it would be to stop breathing. And if you already did, get that gray matter out of storage and rev it up.

There *are* differences in how we use our minds as we age, but they are strategy choices not competency levels. Harkness noted typists at 60 will read ahead in the text and use fewer keystrokes to get the task done while younger typists have more speed but do more work than their older counterparts to achieve the same result.

Some of the stuff about memory challenges makes basic sense. We have more stored information as we get older—simply because we've had more time to accumulate it. It's logical that the challenge of accessing the piece you need is going to be greater. Memory issues are real—but also a matter of practice and what you assume you can do. My dad still remembered the names of the guys he served with in the infantry in WWII when he was 84.

NOT LOSING IT

There are many ways to use your mind in retirement. Work, of course, offers the greatest volume of opportunity. Doing what you already have extensive knowledge of keeps you thinking as you draw from that knowledge. Doing your old work in a new context demands you also learn the context, which ups the intellectual ante. The steepest learning curve will, of course, be if you decide to learn, and then do, something totally new. All great ways to keep your mind in shape.

But there are other options. In a recent piece for *AARP*, Rosabeth Moss Kanter proposed a whole new process that involves going back to school to prepare for roles as community leaders. She, along with others at Harvard University, is developing the concept of Advanced Leadership Schools: "a new stage of higher education—call it even higher education—that turns experience into significance and produces a pool of much needed leaders to improve communities, nations, and the planet. Higher education can redefine later life as a time for social entrepreneurship and public service." We don't all have to go to Harvard for this. If we head to the local community college to take leadership classes or just plain start to lead, we're going to be *thinking*.

Hobbies make you think. Making something with wood or cloth involves engineering. Designing a new garden area requires figuring out the materials and then the plants to get the effect you want. Cooking makes you think in lots of ways—where to find an exotic ingredient; what to substitute if you can't find it; how to keep what you're preparing fresh until time to eat it (particularly fun on an outing); and, of course, just plain following the recipe. Hanging out with your grandkids can help you think—at least if you are open to what they want to talk about.

Ah, now there's an issue. Openness. Thinking in the same ruts using old information you haven't validated in a while is about a much exercise as opening the door to let the cat out. There is thinking and there is THINKING. Remove the fences in your mind. If that little voice is telling you "Oh, I could never do that," keep thinking about doing it. *How* could you do it? Why *can't* you do it? What is really stopping you and is there a way around that? No fences. And no ceilings either. Not letting yourself think the big thoughts is a tragic waste of potential. Or, as Nelson Mandela puts it, "Your playing small does not serve the world."

Being able to think well is going to make you a better problem solver, for sure. But it will also open up a whole new world if you decide not to stay within the boundaries of what you've already experienced. Gather information wherever you can. Read stuff you usually don't. Look at things when you are near them. Talk to people. We used to go to the Colorado State Fair every year. We learned all sorts of cool stuff—like how to make custom saddles and what it takes to raise longhorn cattle in Southern Colorado—just by starting conversations.

Community involvement is another place where you might be able to think. But on that one, you are going to have to choose wisely. Many volunteer situations start with mindless duties that are the exact opposite of what you need. This is a sad statement of non-profits' ability to use the talent they attract but it is a very real problem. If you hope to meet other than intellectual needs with your commitment, this may still work fine. But if you are looking for mental stimulation, be sure you are going to get it before you commit hours a week to a cause that could have you stuffing envelopes alone in a corner or filling water glasses by yourself out in the kitchen.

Be aware there are different KINDS of thinking, too. Drawing from the work of Howard Gardner, Thomas Armstrong describes seven different kinds of intelligence in his book *7 Kinds of Smart*. He lists words, pictures, music, body, logic, people, and self as specific kinds of intelligence. Though we all have preferred kinds of intelligence, we also have potential to develop the others. This is not limited to what we choose in our youth. There are numerous examples of "late blooming intelligence." Grandma Moses was 78 when she gained acclaim as a painter. Harriet Doerr was in her 70s when she penned the acclaimed novel *Stones for Ibarra*—as part of her college coursework.

Sometimes, it's about taking care of other responsibilities before you allow the more creative aspects to gain purchase. Jean Auel had an MBA and a job as the credit manager for an electronics firm when she came across a news article about the possible co-existence of Neanderthal and Cro-Magnon man. Then in her 40s, she decided to try to create a short story from that. The result was *Clan of the Cave Bear* and four other novels in the series, which have sold tens of millions of copies.

In addition to the content areas Armstrong describes, there are a variety of processes involved in thinking. These processes are deliciously, invisibly complex. When you take in information, you must comprehend it initially, assess its validity, categorize and store it, and be able to access it when you want to use it again. When you recall it, you most likely will be integrating it with other information and applying it to come up with an answer you need that goes beyond the original information. What fun.

Thinking is a right and a privilege. Why give it up?

There's another aspect that needs mention here. Guys and creative work. Once they reach adolescence, men are not encouraged to be creative unless they are pursuing it as a profession (and sometimes not even then). This is such a tragedy. Creativity is so good for us on so many levels.

This was brought home for me a few days ago. I was pulling out "things" to describe my son's younger years that we were going to display as part of his wedding. This is my jock son. My finance guy. As I went through the stuff from grade and high school, I discovered the awards he won for both art and creative writing. He's not using that side of himself now. Jocks don't draw and finance guys don't write short stories. I hope he rediscovers it eventually. What he did in school is worth developing. Maybe he will find that out before he reaches 60. That would be nice.

But often, guys never do get back to it. They decide they are *not* creative instead. I think maybe this is the same phenomenon as girls "acting dumb" because it was expected of us in junior high. Men, I beg you, *please* explore the creative pursuits that appeal to you once you have the time. The world needs your vision of beauty.

It's not about how good you are at it. It's about how good you feel doing it—or even learning to do it. If it ignites your passion, you will become good at it as you learn more.

WRITE ON

We are all creative. How we are creative is what makes us each unique. It may be in the kitchen or the garden or the way you deal with the car's dead battery. But you are creative.

Creativity is the ability to come up with something that wasn't there before—be it a watercolor or how to keep fleas off the dog. Creating is a cross between work and play—at least if you are doing it seriously. Creating is deliriously uplifting and mind-numbingly scary. It's a tough gig, which is why it's so damn fun.

Many of us are yearning for a more creative life by the time we are able to retire. Quite often this translates into "becoming a writer." This is, at a minimum, a way to soften the idea that you are stepping away from work. "Being a writer" means you can dabble at this and that and still tell yourself you have a career. You are, after all, "gathering material." That is the fantasy you start with anyway. At least I did.

Writing—what a murky mud puddle. It can be used so many different ways. Writing can be immensely therapeutic. Writing about things that bother you or wounded you or hold you back quite often gives you the strength to let go of them and better live in the moment. This is important writing but not mental writing. And it is probably not writing anyone will ever see unless your kids come across it when they are filling the dumpster after you die.

Writing can also be spiritual—where you let whatever the pen marks turn into be what you had to say. That's not mental writing either; we'll go into that more in Chapter Seven.

For now, let's talk about writing you do with your mind. Most often, intellectual writing is undertaken with the expectation it's going to be shared and maybe even published. It might be the textbook you never quite found the time to do before or a short story, travel piece, novel, or well-structured, carefully rhymed poem. It might be a family history. It might be a blog. The thing to be clear about with intellectual writing is why you are doing it. Because it's very hard to get passion into anything that comes exclusively from your mind. If you have a clear sense of why you need to write it, it will be a lot easier to keep going. (*Please* trust me on this!)

It's also important to understand and respect what you are NOT doing. Some "mental writing" is a community effort. Right now, I'm doing the first draft of a community plan for public art for the city where I live. Our job is to take the information we gathered from the community and use it to create a plan for having art that reflects who we are. When I'm done with the draft, several others on the team will rework either all or specific sections to make it better. The result will be "writing by committee." That's what we need in this case since what we are looking to create is a set of practical guidelines, procedures, and resources for the city to use in having public art.

If I'd have tried to write this book "by committee," it would have been another "60-page abortion." Writing by committee will, by definition, take out both the spontaneity and quirkiness—the personality of the piece. In your personal writing, that would be a great loss. For a group effort, it's inevitable.

So know what you're trying to do. If you want to express *yourself* in the writing, do not give it to everyone you know and ask them to tell you how to make it better. Give it to a few wise people who will let you be who you are but tell you what works and what doesn't. If you are trying to get an accurate set of guidelines developed for an off leash dog park, it's entirely different. Conciseness, clarity, and completeness can often be improved by having a variety of people working to get the words right—at least if they are all trying to do the same thing with the piece.

In many instances, the content area is what will be most demanding mentally. If you choose to write a history of your hometown, finding all the facts you need is going to keep you thinking. Making sure all the facts mesh—or explaining why they don't—will keep you thinking. Getting things in the proper sequence will keep you thinking.

But there are also certain forms of writing that are particularly demanding mentally because of the context in which they are to be used. Screenplays, for example.

To be commercial, a screenplay must be between 95 and 120 pages long. It must be formatted the way people in the industry are accustomed to reading them. (Hurray for software.) Certain happenings have to be set up by certain points in the script because that's what moviegoers have come to expect. And you have to write predominantly in *images*. (Believe it or not, the dialogue is secondary.) All this is on top of the need to write a compelling story about a sympathetic character who faces both an external and an internal challenge. Then, of course, there's the little matter of getting it produced with the right cast and director such that it somewhat resembles what you originally wrote. If you love complexity, this is your gig.

Writing seems like an easy answer to "what do I want to do next." If you are planning to see your work published or produced, there's a lot more to it than sitting at the beach with a pen and a yellow pad. Learn the craft. Read books. Take classes. Do seminars. Join a guild or association of writers. Talk to other writers, especially successful ones. Start doing this *before* you retire. Long before if possible. Becoming a writer is a life-long effort

And last but not least, the part of writing that most demands rational thought is the business end. If you want to do it for money, you have a lot to learn about how that segment of industry works. That's not bad. It's one more way to keep you thinking.

And that is the bottom line for how to keep your mind as you age. USE IT.

Think and Do

When I started work on this chapter, we were celebrating the Fourth of July. The local paper printed a sample version of the test immigrants are required to pass before they can become citizens of the United States. Each time I've worked on this chapter, I've vacillated between taking this exercise out and leaving it in. I decided to leave it in—I'll explain why after you work on it. If you don't want to bother with it, skip it. But it was an eye opener for me—and it does make you use your head.

Exercise 5.1—A CITIZEN'S TEST
(Optional if you were born a US citizen....)

How much do you know of what the government
expects prospective citizens to know?

1. What are the colors of our flag?

2. What do the stars on the flag mean?

3. How many stars are there on our flag?

4. What color are the stars on our flag?

5. How many stripes are there on the flag?

6. What do the stripes on the flag mean?

7. What colors are the stripes on the flag?

8. How many states are there in the Union (the United States)?

9. What do we celebrate on the Fourth of July?

10. Independence Day celebrates independence from whom?

11. What country did we fight during the Revolutionary War?

12. Who was the first president of the United States?

13. Who is the president of the United States today?

14. Who is the vice president of the United States today?

15. Who elects the president of the United States?

16. Who becomes president if the president dies?

17. What is the Constitution?

18. What do we call changes to the Constitution?

19. How many changes, or amendments, are there to the Constitution?

20. What are the three branches of our government?

21. What is the legislative branch of our government?

22. What makes up Congress?

23. Who makes the federal laws in the United States?

24. Who elects Congress?

25. How many senators are there in Congress?

26. For how long is a senator elected?

27. Name two senators from your state.

28. How many voting members are there in the House of Representatives?

29. For how long do we elect each member of the House of Representatives?

30. Who is the head of the executive branch of the US government?

31. For how long is the president elected?

32. What is the highest part of the judiciary branch of the U.S. government?

33. What are the duties of the Supreme Court?

34. What is the Supreme Law of the United States?

35. What is the Bill of Rights?

36. What is the capital of the state you live in?

37. Who is the current governor of the state you live in?

38. Who becomes president if both the president and the vice president die?

39. Who is the chief justice of the Supreme Court?

40. What were the original 13 states?

41. Who said, "Give me liberty or give me death?"

42. Name some countries that were our enemies in World War II.

43. What was the 49th state added to our Union (the United States)?

44. How many full terms can a president serve?

45. Who was Martin Luther King, Jr.?

46. What are some to the requirements to be eligible to become president?

47. Why are there 100 senators in the United States Senate?

48. Who nominates judges for the Supreme Court?

49. How many Supreme Court judges are there?

50. Why did the Pilgrims come to America?

51. What is the executive of a state government called?

52. What is the head executive of a city government called?

53. What holiday was celebrated for the first time by American colonists?

54. Who was the main writer of the Declaration of Independence?

55. When was the Declaration of Independence adopted?

56. What are some of the basic beliefs of the Declaration of Independence?

57. What is the national anthem of the United States?

58. Who wrote "The Star Spangled Banner?"

59. What is the minimum voting age in the United States?

60. Who signs bills into law?

61. What is the highest court in the United States?

62. Who was president during the Civil War?

63. What did the Emancipation Proclamation do?

64. What special group advises the president?

65. Which president is called the Father of our Country?

66. Which president was the first commander in chief of the U.S. Army and Navy?

67. What was the 50th state to be added to our Union (the United States)?

68. Who helped the Pilgrims in America?

69. What is the name of the ship that brought the Pilgrims to America?

70. What were the 13 original states of the United States called before they were states?

71. What group has the power to declare war?

72. Name the Amendments that guarantee or address voting rights.

73. In what year was the Constitution written?

74. What are the 10 amendments to the Constitution called?

75. Whose rights are guaranteed by the Constitution and the Bill of Rights?

76. What is the introduction to the Constitution called?

77. Who meets in the U.S. Capitol building?

78. What is the name of the president's official home?

79. Where is the White House located?

80. Name one right or freedom guaranteed by the First Amendment.

81. Who is the commander in chief of the United States military?

82. In what month do we vote for the president?

83. In what month is a new president inaugurated?

84. How many times may a senator or a congressman be re-elected?

85. What are the two major political parties in the United States today?

86. What is the executive branch of our government?

87. Where does freedom of speech come from?

88. What U.S. Citizenship and Immigration form is used to apply for naturalized citizenship?

89. What kind of government does the United States have?

90. Name one of the purposes of the United Nations.

91. Name one benefit of being a citizen of the United States.

92. Can the Constitution be changed?

93. What is the most important right granted to United States citizens?

94. What is the White House?

95. What is the United States Capitol?

96. How many branches are there in the United States government?

Answers

1. Red, white and blue

2. One for each state

3. There are 50 stars on our flag.

4. The stars in the flag are white.

5. There are 13 stripes on our flag.

6. The first 13 states.

7. The stripes on the flag are red and white.

8. 50 states

9. Independence Day

10. Independence from Great Britain

11. We fought Great Britain in the Revolutionary War

12. George Washington

13. George W. Bush

14. Dick Cheney

15. The Electoral College

16. The vice president

17. The supreme law of the land.

18. Amendments

19. 27 amendments

20. Executive, judicial and legislative

21. Congress

22. The Senate and the House of Representatives

23. Congress

24. The citizens of the United States

25. There are 100 senators in Congress, two from each state

26. Six years

27. Maria Cantwell and Patty Murray (for Washington state in 2006)

28. There are 435 voting members in the House of Representatives

29. For two years

30. The president

31. The president is elected for four years.

32. The Supreme Court

33. To interpret and explain the laws

34. The Constitution

35. The first 10 amendments to the Constitution

36. Olympia (for Washington state)

37. Christine Gregoire (for Washington state in 2006.)

38. The Speaker of the House

39. John G. Roberts, Jr.

40. Virginia, Massachusetts, Maryland, Rhode Island, Connecticut, New Hampshire, North Carolina, South Carolina, New York, New Jersey, Pennsylvania, Delaware, and Georgia.

41. Patrick Henry

42. Germany, Italy, and Japan

43. Alaska

44. Two full terms

45. A civil rights leader

46. A candidate for president must be a native-born—not naturalized—citizen, be at least 35 years old and have lived in the U.S. for at least 14 years.

47. Each state elects two senators.

48. The president nominates judges for the Supreme Court.

49. There are nine Supreme Court judges.

50. To gain religious freedom.

51. The governor

52. The mayor

53. Thanksgiving

54. Thomas Jefferson

55. July 4, 1776

56. That all men are created equal and have the right to life, liberty, and the pursuit of happiness

57. The Star Spangled Banner

58. Francis Scott Key

59. 18 is the minimum voting age.

60. The president

61. The Supreme Court

62. Abraham Lincoln

63. The Emancipation Proclamation freed the slaves.

64. The Cabinet advises the president.

65. George Washington

66. George Washington

67. Hawaii

68. American Indians

69. The Mayflower

70. Colonies

71. Congress has the power to declare war.

72. The 15th, 19th, 24th and 26th amendments.

73. The Constitution was written in 1787.

74. The Bill of Rights

75. All people living in the United States

76. The Preamble

77. Congress

78. The White House

79. Washington, D.C.

80. The rights of freedom of religion, of speech, of the press, of assembly, and to petition the government

81. The president

82. November

83. January

84. There is no limit.

85. The Democratic and Republican parties

86. The president, the Cabinet and departments under the Cabinet members

87. The Bill of Rights

88. Form N-400 (Application for Naturalization)

89. A republic

90. For countries to discuss and try to resolve world problems or to provide economic aid to many countries

91. To obtain federal government jobs, to travel with a U.S. passport or to petition for close relatives to come to the United States to live

92. Yes, the Constitution can be changed.

93. The right to vote

94. The president's official home

95. The place where Congress meets

96. There are three branches.

This is an interesting version of "smart." People seem to like this kind of thing just to see if they can come up with the right answer. When friends leafed through the manuscript, they'd get to this exercise and read the questions out loud to each other. That's one reason I included it. People have fun with it.

But unless you are preparing to take the citizenship test for real, there is no negative consequence to not knowing these answers. And that's the other reason it's in here—to help make that point. There's nothing wrong with not having immediate answers to questions that don't affect your daily life—especially if you know where to look them up. There's everything wrong with not knowing the stuff it really is in your best interest to comprehend.

At this point in our lives, it's too easy to be forgiven when we don't WANT to learn things. Like how to put phone numbers in the new cell phone or get the remote to talk to the new TV or sign up for part D of

Medicare. Staying ignorant on this kind of stuff is not a good idea. If at all possible, LEARN the things you need to know to make your life work the best it can. Sure, this stuff can be boring, frustrating and even humiliating. Sure learning it is not as much fun as seeing who "survives" on whatever reality show is on. But it is essential that you make the effort to learn it for two reasons. It is stuff you DO need to know. And it is stuff that makes you think.

If you are telling yourself you "just don't get it" and using your age as an excuse not to learn, get real. It's not age that's holding you back. It's your attitude. There are folks in their 90's getting college degrees. Don't tell me you're too old to think.

Exercise 5.2—WHERE THE ACTION IS

With a set routine and regular activities, things run on automatic pilot pretty easily. It's important to find ways to think and to hang out with people who MAKE you think.

Look for fun ways to use your mind. Thinking is as important as breathing. And just like with breathing, some environments make it easier than others. Use this exercise to assess how much your lifestyle offers ways to keep yourself mentally sharp.

Right now, the most complex thinking I do is: _____

_____

_____

I like (don't like) this thinking because: _____

_____

_____

When I watch television, I keep my mind active by: _____

_____

_____

My smartest friend challenges my thinking by: _____

_____

_____

Ways I can get more mental exercise: _____

_____

_____

The topics I like most to think about are: _____

_____

_____

The complexity of those topics: _____

_____

_____

The people or things in my life that think for me when I should be thinking for myself are: _____

_____

_____

The ways I keep myself thinking right now: _____

_____

_____

Overall, I'd rate my commitment to keeping myself sharp mentally as:

_____

_____

We have a long way to go to get to where we *encourage* each other to think instead of relying on information, conclusions, and decisions provided by others. Some things do need to be done by those who are more specifically competent. This is as true for the person who cuts my hair as it is for the person I pay to manage my finances. Being unique means being inept at some things. But that doesn't remove your responsibility to think, even in those arenas. I am still "the boss of my hair." And I still need to pay attention to what my money manager has accomplished if I am going to do a good job of taking care of myself.

CONFESSIONS OF A COMPLEX PLAYBABY

Okay, I admit it. I look for complexity. When I can't find it, I make it—usually without meaning to. This is particularly true of how I've been playing for the last 10 years.

Quilting is a fairly complex hobby, so I tried that. It is complex. Find the right pattern and the fabrics to give it "punch." Cut the pieces precisely and in the right directions. Sew them together the right way. Press the seams so they lay correctly. Baste the batt between the top and the backing. And finally, sew a pattern all over the top/batt/backing sandwich to "quilt" it. Plenty of complexity, right?

Nope. After I'd learned the basics—including my discovery of that awesome tool, the rotary cutter—I had to add something to stay interested.

So I started dyeing my own fabric. That was huge fun. It was kinda like Christmas every time I started rinsing what I'd scrunched up, twisted and otherwise manipulated. I never knew what was going to emerge from the dye bath. Each piece of fabric was a different Technicolor fantasy. Lots of shadows and feathery variations, lots of color shading.

But I needed more. I started dyeing other things. Queen-sized sheets (not recommended). T-shirts. Socks. Scarves. A sarong. I finally found something I could stay with when I started hemming napkins and dyeing those. I think I have 20 of them—and I've given a bunch away. I use them. People love them because they are both soft and interesting. But every once in a while, I decide to re-dye them. Just to see what happens.

When I moved into this house, I decided I needed a big wall quilt for the landing. I wanted to use a technique called strip quilting that doesn't rely on a pattern at all. You sew bands and bands and bands of fabric together into a tube, cut strips off the tube, and open each strip at a different place get a pattern on the quilt top that's like a wave. Thinking about what that next strip was going to do to the emerging design was the best part of the fun. But once I'd mastered the technique, I needed new grist. I moved outside.

The garden I'd just acquired needed major surgery—or so I thought. Existing plants were in the wrong places. Existing hardscape wouldn't work for what I wanted. I told myself I needed to figure out the light and moisture situation in the different parts of the yard before I actually started changing things. That lasted about three months. Then I couldn't stand it—I needed a complex project and the yard was the most promising candidate.

I moved 20 thyme plants to a stubborn hillside. They died anyway, but I acquired a helluva set of biceps. I replanted all the dianthus from where I wanted vegetables to the front garden. I moved clematis that were too close to the house to a trellis in a fenced corner I hated mowing. I moved lilies so I could plant strawberries.

Then I got serious and spent money. I replaced the old patio—which resembled a landing strip—with a curving expanse of exposed aggregate. I had to explain what I wanted to the concrete guys five times. When they finished it, they claimed it as if they'd invented it. "Why do you want to do *curves*?" became "We sure came up with a great shape, didn't we?"

Another area, above some pretty steps made out of decking, ended in a pier into nothing. A second patio solved that. Yep. Curved. Then it was the pond lady's turn. The water feature is perfect—both in how it looks and how it sounds.

It was finally planting time. Whooo hoo! My former husband is correct. I've never met a plant I didn't like. Well, close. I'm really sick of petunias. I've been planting this yard for two years now. It's pretty and a great place to relax, but there are a few more touches to get it finished. So it continues to be great exercise—mental as well as physical.

The most recent "complexity project" was a partnership with my brother Steve. My siblings are equally afflicted with a need for complexity. (This particular brother copied the entire evolutionary tree in eighth grade—by hand.)

The game started when he and I went to Portland, Oregon overnight as a way to kick off our Christmas shopping. We didn't buy any gifts—we didn't make it past the toy store downtown—Little Finnegan's. They sell silly stuff for adults. We were definitely in a silly mood. We found little plastic finger puppet nuns that looked just like the order who taught the entire family first grade through senior year of high school. I have six siblings. Three of them are sisters who still live in Wisconsin. Steve and I decided they needed nuns. We each bought four. One for each of these three sisters plus one to keep.

Then we went to dinner. And started drinking wine. On the second—large—glass, we came up with the Nun-of-the-Month Club. Each of our three sisters would get a nun every month for a year. We went back to Little Finnegan's the next morning and bought a whole lot more nuns.

By the time we'd driven back to Tacoma, just mailing the little plastic nuns each month seemed too simple. The nuns needed names—and personalities. We decided to write biographies for each one. Then we concocted a baseball-card format, with the nun—complete with her number—glued to the corner of a card that included stats and other information. Steve found a website with a long list of patron saints for really weird stuff—like vinegar makers and arms dealers—that helped immensely. We were into the project in earnest.

Sort of. Life intervened. We worked on bios. January became February—no nuns had gone out. We worked on bios. February became March. We decided the sibling sisters would receive a trial membership instead of a whole year. And that we would send four nuns at a time to each sister—so they would still each get 12. We were planning on sending them anonymously. So I had to have nuns, too—to be able to talk the talk if any of them asked me about nuns.

We finally did send a batch. We knew if they saw a Tacoma postmark, they'd be onto us. So we weighed them and put postage on them and sent them off to a friend in Minneapolis to mail for us. Bless her, she did. It was the perfect diversionary city. One of the sisters has a daughter in

Minneapolis and all three have friends there. The finger of accusation would certainly point elsewhere.

They arrived at the sisters' mailboxes on April Fools Day. I wish we could say we planned that.

Within minutes, Steve got an e-mail from our youngest sister, thanking him for the joke. At least MY part in it hadn't been assumed. He's the quiet one. He's the overworked one. Why did they blame him? I don't know, but I will remember that for whatever mischief I decide to perpetrate next.

Steve forwarded her note to me—as well as the ones that came soon after from the other two sisters—so I knew what they were saying. We discussed strategy. There was only one real option—lie like hell. So Steve sent out a smoke screen. He did such a good job at it that even I believed him. I sent him an e-mail reply to his copy to me—trying to cheer him up about what he told my sisters to throw them off track.

Oh the joy of complexity! My oldest sister eventually decided I was the culprit. She sent me a shirt and vowed to send one every month—each rattier than the last—until I confessed. Nope.

In a blink, it was time to do the next batch. We opted to try a double blind nun drop. Steve mailed a letter from Paducah, Kentucky (on a layover that was part of a circuitous plane trip to Wisconsin from Seattle). The very official stationery offered our oldest sister's middle kid the chance to participate by mailing a package to his mother and aunts from North Carolina. (His family is the lone outpost of our clan in that state.) But he didn't know who was inviting him into the mischief. He was to reply to "Mr. Redd" in San Diego who was actually a friend of Steve's. "Mr. Redd" was to let Steve know via e-mail if the reply card arrived. It did, but his e-mail was broken so we didn't know we had a go.

In the meantime, our North Carolina accomplice had been forced to swear his 10-year-old son to secrecy after the boy read the letter of invitation over his dad's shoulder. Even the dead ends were getting complicated. Of course, the kid blabbed to his grandma anyway. Perfect!

We resorted to Plan B for Batch 2. I asked a friend in Texas to mail them. He did. But he wasn't sure which city they would be postmarked from. I was frantic. The postmark might be a key point when my sisters talked nuns with me on this round. Keeping up the ruse was going to be dicey without knowing what it said on their envelopes.

Not a problem. None of the sisters said *anything*. This was an excellent strategy on their part—it drove both Steve and me nuts. Eventually I inquired of my youngest sister. She replied that she'd gotten them and that it must be the "nun-of-every-other-month club" since they'd arrived in June. I guess we deserved that.

Around then, we decided we were tired of writing nuns' biographies. We resorted to Plan X. We mailed each sister a letter saying there was a nun shortage and suggested if they wanted any more of these precious remembrances, they were available for $50 each. No takers. But we gave our oldest brother's address as the clearinghouse and copied him on the letter. He got the copy on his birthday. He thought the joke was just for him. I wish I could say we planned that, too.

We finally came clean about the whole thing at a family picnic in August. At which point the third generation (grandkids) began flying the nuns in Styrofoam airplanes purchased for the occasion. So the complexity veered in the direction of aerodynamics. Cool.

The point of all this is that play can also be a great source of mental gymnastics. Using your mind is no different than using your other muscles. If you work them every chance you get, they stay strong and serve you well.

Chapter Six:

Marshmallows, Icicles, and Prickly Things in the Dark

A FEW MONTHS AFTER I'D MOVED INTO THE HOUSE I live in now, I was taking out the garbage. It wasn't any kind of special garbage. It wasn't even garbage day. I was just taking out the garbage because the bag was full. As I dumped the cinched sack of orange peels, junk mail, and empty cartons in the trash can, I heard someone say "I am so happy."

I was startled to realize it was me. I'd been chasing after happiness for 58 years and here it was, holding the garbage can lid. What changed?

I'd started being me—being truthful and complete about what I needed, liked, wanted, and felt. I didn't *have* a lot of it. My source of livelihood was uncertain. I'd decided to "take a year off from guys" which meant I didn't have someone right there to have fun with. My financial advisor wasn't doing what I needed. It was November in the Pacific Northwest—the equivalent of sitting in a leaky clothes hamper in the shower for thirty days. And still there I was, totally content and infinitely pleased with my life.

Sometimes, it's best just to live it and not worry about why you lucked into what you have.

One of the greatest benefits of reaching retirement is that we have been through a lot. The possibility something horrible, fantastic, daunting, or exquisite *might* happen was long ago replaced by the real thing. We've *felt* the fear of a cancer scare—or the monster itself. We've *felt* the suffocating blackness of loss—a loved one who left this realm too soon, a lover who decided on someone else, the job we thought only we could do. We've felt the giddiness of regained freedom—after a divorce, the end of an impossible work project, or a debilitating injury. We have felt life. A lot of it. We know about feelings even if we don't talk about them. In fact, by this point, talking about them is often unnecessary. We can sit with someone going through some version of emotional hell and offer great solace by saying nothing at all.

We have perspective. It's not the end of the world when a flight is cancelled or someone we'd hoped to spend time with has to beg off at the last minute. We have made it a long way on the Road of Life. We are survivors. We know pain. We recognize joy. We have felt much. Even the manly men will let the tears come sometimes by the time they get to 60. All this is good. Feeling our feelings is an integral part of being who we are. And "being who we are" is what living well at this stage of life is built on.

We have felt much. Yes. But there is still a lot to do in terms of identifying it and using it to define the best life you can live. Don't worry about labeling what you are feeling as a particular emotion. Worry about *noticing* what you are feeling.

A few months ago, I started to get to know an incredible man. Competent. Strong. Interesting. Independent. Most of what I had on "the list" was part of who he seemed to be. Yet, after one particularly fun day together, I realized I wanted out—to stop seeing him. Immediately. I wanted it desperately. I even tore up "the list."

Resorting to an emotional label might have left me at "not interested." With that, I would have simply backed away. But it made no sense that I would be "not interested." This guy embodied so much that I liked and valued. I needed to go deeper than an easy label to understand what was going on. When I explored the feeling I was really having, I discovered *dread.* At the very bottom of my panic was a sense that I would be back in prison if he became an on-going part of my life.

Getting to that level of understanding about what I was feeling helped me realize it wasn't the guy I had to jettison. It's what I was telling myself that needed revision. I was jumping from "seeing someone" to "being a traditional couple" entirely in my head. He had not said word one to that effect. I'd finally gained my freedom from a very painful version of "being a traditional couple" two years earlier. Of course, the idea of going back to that same set-up would feel like emotional incarceration.

Once I could see I was reacting to my own experience, the dread went away. I didn't have to do that again. I had—and will always have—the right to shape any relationship I choose to be part of. As does whomever I'm relating to. The honesty of living in this moment as who I am (and he is) will, of itself, keep me far away from the thing that hurt so much before.

Basics

There are a few basic things we need to agree on.

- Emotions are part of being human.
- Being aware of them and using them to make good decisions is a personal choice.
- Not everyone is going to make the same choice.

Every human being who has ever walked the earth has had feelings. However, for millennia, they weren't a topic of conversation. Neither were hair follicles or the spleen. The fact that they were not part of the popular map of human functioning even 100 years ago is not a question of the validity of their existence. It's a matter of how far we have been able to progress on that course of investigation. It took us a while to get to where we could map the human genome, too.

Emotions are hard to study. You can't take their dimensions or write out a chemical formula for them. They are not made up of a specific set of elements arranged neatly into a unique set of molecules. As with most things that are just starting to be studied, there are those who claim they aren't real and don't need to be investigated at all. Baloney. Where would we be if the visionaries had not started to figure out electricity? Or DNA?

Emotions are hard to grasp when we experience them, too. That does not make them any less real. For what we are doing here, comprehending them is essential. The amount of work you put into understanding what you are feeling as you consider what to do next will have a major impact on the quality of your life from here on. You can survive while remaining emotionally comatose, but you aren't really alive if you do. Your eyes may *see* the sun peek over the far mountains as you stand in the hills at dawn, but to enjoy that sunrise, you must *feel* it. It's the exhilaration of a new day and the promise of more tomorrows that engender the magnificence of what you are watching. You're seeing it with your *heart*.

Feeling is one of the best parts of getting older. We have plenty of experience to establish perspective and plenty of time to really savor what comes. Even pain means more at this stage of our lives. We have had plenty by this point. Physical pain in injuries and illnesses. Emotional pain in losses we've had to endure that left us hollow and wondering if life could go on. Maybe even spiritual pain as we wandered the bleak aridness of a dark night of the soul. We need to claim the pain we've known—perhaps like battle ribbons. What we've felt before can take us a long way in appreciating and using what we feel now. That makes it easier to learn what the current situation has to teach us.

That said, not everyone is going to do this the same way. In particular, not everyone is going to want to *talk* about feelings. The most tender feelings are like marshmallows. They dry out and get hard if they are exposed to the air for too long. I don't talk about the things that are deepest in my heart much any more. It's not that I don't cherish them enough—or feel them strongly. It's just that having other people know I have them is no longer important. *Feeling* them is.

A while back, a writer friend and I were laughing about the difference between men and women in terms of the traumas of childhood.

She admitted she was finally ready to accept what her husband was telling her as truth—that his childhood had been happy. "Fine," someone tells us and we immediately think "He's just not ready to deal with it." Perhaps he is. Perhaps he has. Perhaps there's nothing to deal with. Or, as Fritz Perls put it, "You be you, and I'll be me."

I'm not so sure we need to go digging into the stinky stuff of the past. It's been a livelihood for counselors for decades, but what do you gain? Spend that time and money working on how you want to live now. That's what's going to get you to a good life.

Some of it has to do with the victim thing. If you want to be a victim, you're gonna need your past. It's such fertile ground for inequity—real or perceived. Someone did something that was unfair to you. Someone did something unspeakable. Someone did something that scarred you for the rest of your life. Hard as it is to hear, all of it is your choice. There are those who are scarred for life simply because they were the middle child. Yet there are also those who managed to survive death camps with a lightness of spirit that makes you believe in angels. What you decide to focus on is up to you. Do you want to be happy now or do you want to be the aggrieved party of some previous situation so that people feel sorry for you?

Being able to and comfortable at figuring out your feelings is incredibly empowering. Perhaps you're already good at it. For most of us, this area of knowledge has been a hit-and-miss proposition. The breadth of experience we can now claim gives us a strong platform from which to work. Once we understand what the platform is composed of. You still have to *commit* to learning what's there. To decide to explore that territory.

Guys in particular have skittered away from "feelings" since they learned "big boys don't cry." Getting to the bottom of what you are feeling and using that information in your decision-making can supercharge your effectiveness in making life and lifestyle choices. But it's still up to you. *Are you willing to go there?* I hope you said "yes." It's a better ride.

There are four emotions we need to touch on specifically. Before we do that, I want to touch on something more general. This is fairly mainstream western thinking. It has to do with the link between attitude and emotion. I just went through a bout with it recently that also reminded me: Attitude is where stress comes into the picture.

At the moment, I have a lot to do. This is good in most ways. As I have already acknowledged, I need a high level of activity. But for some reason, I decided I didn't want to have to do one of the projects I'd committed to. It was a big project, and I just kept obsessing about not wanting to do it.

Within a couple days, I was thinking the most amazing range of negative thoughts. I didn't want to do any of the things I needed to get done. I was mad at everybody, from my brother to the woman in front of me at the post office. These people had not suddenly gotten impossible to deal with. I had just bought in on a negative mindset. And the race to convert *everything* I thought about to that same currency was swift.

Within a few days of the start of the negative thinking, I started to have indigestion—one of my first signs of stress. At the same time, I started being fearful—something I had not felt since I left my bad marriage. I tell you this as if I knew what was going on as it was happening. I didn't. But when my gut started to scream for the attention it deserved, the predicament came into blessedly clear focus. I needed to let go of what I was thinking about that one project. Or my life was not going to be any fun.

A negative attitude will not just ruin dinner with friends or an adult child's visit—though those are bad enough. That kind of mental state can make you sick. It can also make you not want to do what you need to do to get out of the funk because "you're afraid." Don't go there. When your find yourself getting negative, get to the root of it and change your thinking to get back on the sunny side. Negativity can be *lethal*.

ANGER

There are several emotions that have enough impact to warrant being addressed specifically. The first is anger. In many households, including the one I grew up in, anger is quite acceptable. In fact, it was the only emotion regularly expressed in my family of origin. We would defend each other to the death if necessary out in the "World." But we never admitted it to each at home. We all had stiletto tongues and quick minds and were quite ready to draw sibling emotional blood whenever we thought we needed to.

It never occurred to us the verbal attacks weren't appropriate. It took me until I was in my 40s and holding an executive level job to learn this is NOT the way the rest of world works. The book *When Anger Hurts* by Matthew McKay, Peter Rogers, and Judith McKay was a wake-up call with a bullhorn for me. I was stunned at the damage I was doing with my angry outbursts. The level of destruction I'd caused in my personal relationships was devastating.

I was extremely lucky. I learned this without a heart attack, a stroke, or the permanent alienation of someone I loved. I learned it reading a book in the safety and comfort of my family room. These days, you might learn it on the highway, looking down the barrel of a semi-automatic pistol drawn in road rage.

Anger is an essential emotion. There are things we *need* to get angry about. I am angry now about how invisible we become to the greater society when we retire. I am angry so many of us have been so disenfranchised by a society focused on youth instead of vibrance. My anger spurs me to action, and I need it. But that's not the same as getting mad because someone cut in front of me in line at the grocery store.

One of my favorite quotes is "Never attribute to malice what can be explained by ignorance." (Sure wish I could remember who said it.) That quote usually keeps me out of escalating pissing matches. People don't do things to be nasty very often. They do them because they either think it's the right thing to do or they don't think at all. At least most of the time. But even with the authentic jerks, getting mad doesn't help solve the problem. In fact, it makes it harder because when you are angry, it's harder to think. You can't solve anything. Anger makes the problem continue—which is probably why lawyering is such a profitable profession.

You can certainly choose to be angry. You can also choose to throw all your socks out the nearest window. Neither is a particularly useful strategy.

Anger comes easily to the disenfranchised. Find your power, your purpose, and the life you were meant to live and your anger is likely to evaporate.

FEAR

The second emotion I want to address is fear. We need this one, too. We wouldn't have made it past our saber-toothed tiger days as a species if our ancestors had not felt fear. But there is fear, and there is "fear." Fear in the face of actual danger is wise. You *don't* want to walk too close to the edge of a stairway with no railing. You *don't* want to take the shortcut across the valley if you can see a bear browsing there. But being afraid of gray hair, wrinkles, and sagging breasts is silly. So is being afraid of tomorrow.

Fear can either paralyze you or propel you forward. Eleanor Roosevelt advised, "Do at least one thing every day that you're afraid of." I found that quote about the time I started hiking in earnest. It got me across many a footlog plus some scary scree slopes. And still does.

Conquering the fear I feel in those situations gives me confidence I would not have had otherwise. Doing the thing that scares me makes me willing to do something else next that I might not have been able to do otherwise. Fear is not to be ignored. It is to be met. Authentic fear challenges us to go beyond our comfort level—with a skill we need to develop, a risk we need to take, or to find a smart way out of a dangerous situation.

Fake fear is something else. Fake fear is what you experience when you are aiming for impossible control. If you are worrying about things you have no way of affecting, you are not living in fear, you are living under the delusion that you have the right and the responsibility to control everything that happens in your life. Get real. You are *not* General Manager of the Universe. You never will be. Let it go.

LOVE

And then there is love. By now, we all have horror stories about loving someone we would have been wise not to or not being loved by someone we wanted. Romantic love deserves a whole book's worth of discussion. But some of the traumas we experience in romantic love are actually about not knowing how to be ourselves. And not knowing what we want and need. Romantic love is only the tip of the iceberg. We need to step up to love in every context, not just when we yearn for someone to wake up with.

Love is a BIG piece of a good life. Love is connection, acceptance, and contentment. Love is being there for someone else. Love is having that someone else be there when *you* need it. Often, that person will not be your mate. And at this point in our lives, we seem to understand that a little better. Sometimes it's a friend. Sometimes it's a sibling. Sometimes it's a stranger on an airplane who sees what you are going through better than the folks who think they know you well.

Given its magnitude, covering the topic of love here is unrealistic. The thing that makes me want to bring up "love" at all is that we bring it up too often. We claim it when we don't feel it. We say it when we don't mean it. We use the words "I love you" for emotional blackmail more than any other words in the language. Be honest with what you're feeling. Is it love? Or like? Or lust? Or none of the above?

Love is THE marshmallow emotion. Leaving it out in the ordinary air by talking about it ruins it. Feel it. Act on it. Mean it if you say "I love you." But then shut up. Loving someone is deep, strong stuff. Respect your ability to do that. And then just do it. Don't talk about it. Do it—quietly, confidently, gently. Appreciate the love you receive, too—from your partner, your mother, your kids, your dog.

FEELING OLD

The last emotion we need to consider specifically doesn't have a neat label—yet. It's "feeling old." Perhaps we could call it "irrelevance." Perhaps we could call it "perceived incompetence." Perhaps we can just get rid of it and not worry about what to call it at all.

When we leave work, we usually leave the part of life that confirms our competence behind. That regular paycheck said you were competent.

Having a project assigned to you said you were competent. Even the impossible customer demanding the unreasonable yet again sent the message that you were able to get that job done. If he didn't think you could fix it, he wouldn't have bothered to call and complain.

"Feeling old" is a choice. Sometimes we make it so automatically we don't realize we've done it. I felt old when I got an AARP card—at the age of 40, as the spouse of someone who'd just turned 50 and loved to save a buck. I felt old when I had to help him carry his luggage. I felt old when I spent my time with friends he'd chosen who were even older than he. But it was still my choice to feel old. I don't do that any more.

Even if you are 110, you do not have to *feel* old. Often, that feeling old thing is a smoke screen. It's a way of justifying not doing what scares you. You're not old. You're chicken. Now go do it.

"The Important People"

The other big emotional deal we need to get clear on is relationships. Who do you want in your life now and who do you need to let go of?

Simply put, you want more time with the people who energize you by their presence. You want less time with the toxic crowd—the people who drag you down with their whining and woe. This gets tricky though, because making it this far doesn't mean all the negative people in your life are just going to get on the train for somewhere else.

The more complex answer to the question revolves around understanding your own emotions. Impossible people are part of life. And sometimes they are folks you have to be around a lot. But if you know they are a drain, you can take precautions and devise strategies to help yourself stay positive when you are with them.

PARENTS

For those of us whose parents are still part of the picture, this time can be far more challenging. We're accustomed to having our parents be the strong ones, the capable ones. Yet as they move into advanced age, this might not be the case. There's beauty in the symmetry of the very young and the very old requiring the loving care of others, but it's not as easy to see if you are the one who has to provide all that loving care. With babies, you know the timeline. In a few years they will be walking and talking and in a few more years after that they will be off to kindergarten…high school…college.

With loved ones in advanced age, we are working in the dark. We have no idea whether we are looking at a month or 10 years of the care we are being asked to give. It could change drastically and become even more demanding overnight. This lack of predictability makes the responsibility far more stressful. In classic psychology experiments, researchers found that participants who knew what to expect could endure significantly more than those who didn't. In fact, the need to control the situation was significantly lower for those who could predict what was going to happen.

The responsibilities with parents as they age can be daunting. Those responsibilities can also be shared. Often that is not done at all or not done well though. Those who handle the day-to-day care are appreciated (hopefully)—and left to do it. We need more community resources to help with this challenge, but we also need stronger backbones. If you are a caregiver and are stretched too thin, look to the others in your parent's circle for help. Your siblings and other relatives, of course, but also friends and church members. Let the others help so you can keep your own vibrance. Let the others help because helping is good and we all need and want to do good.

KIDS

If you're still raising young children, I am surprised you're reading this. Amazed you have time, actually. Bless you and have fun. What I need to say about kids here is mostly about the older ones.

First, let's talk about the ones who went out on their own and then moved back home to make ends meet. And the ones who have their own places and are raising families, but want you to drop everything when they need a sitter. The adult kids who are still expecting their folks to carry whatever they can't.

You're not the local help mission. If they can't pay rent in money, they can certainly pay it in labor to keep the house up. Their kids are *their* responsibility. Love the grandbabies and cherish your time with them. But being at the beck and call of their parents is a disservice to yourself and the young family. If you solve every problem for them, they never learn how. At some point, there will be something that makes it impossible for you to continue the service. And then they are going to have big problems if you haven't given them room to figure things out.

Relating to kids at this stage is more challenging than one might expect. They usually are trying to live their own lives. Often, that means you don't see as much of them in yours as you'd like. What a relief when I finally realized my boys' lack of presence in my life was proof of my proficiency as a mother. I've parented two children to successful adulthood. They are both doing things that benefit the world. They are good partners and good employees. They help their friends, neighbors, and extended families. That makes them very busy. They check-in from time to time to see how I'm doing. That's enough. It took a while for me to figure that out.

The other thing is to make sure they know who you really are. My kids never got the full strength version of the Real Me until the last two years. My energy level now is higher than when they lived with me and has been a surprise them. But this version of me is authentic. It's the one that makes me happy. They know I'm not looking for the rocking chair. When they call, I might be hiking or at a meeting. This weekend, I might be going to a movie or on a mule pack trip. They are happy I have a life. When I was feeling sorry for myself because "they never call," I was telling myself I didn't (have a life) and that they needed to pay more attention to me. That is serious baloney. Don't do it.

So…if you are thinking you will have a lot more time to do things with your kids when you retire, you may want to assess *their* availability before you chart that course. They are not retired. The likelihood they can and want to spend large amounts of their time, money or both with their parents needs to be established rather than assumed.

GRANDCHILDREN

And then there are the *grandkids*. This it totally unique territory. One of my friends hosts her five granddaughters for a week every summer so they can participate in vacation Bible school together. She is smart about knowing when to split them up. She is smart about knowing what she is getting into. But she is still exhausted at the end of that week. "Grandma camp" is fun for her, but she knows it's going to take a toll.

That's probably the most important thing to know about grandparenting. It's not all cute. But it's not all fatigue either—though you can get bone tired at it. My aunt still takes care of her youngest son's three school-age boys on a regular basis. She's 85. Her life would have far less meaning without the kids in it. If you want to see "vibrant," ask my Aunt Lou to smile.

Grandchildren are the light of our lives in many cases. The relationships built between active grandparents and growing grandkids can be downright awesome. But they are a function of the specifics of that situation, not a given. For some of us, babysitting the grand-dog might be as close as we get to that kind of relationship.

These are things that evolve, not things you can orchestrate. Being who you are and finding all the other things that bring you joy and satisfaction gives them room to develop without being forced. Setting boundaries on how much you are available to help is wise. Kids are used to Mom and Dad taking care of things. That doesn't mean you have to—or should—every time they ask. Pay attention to what's going on in your own life, too. What they need is important, but so is what you need.

And believe them when they tell you they want to do it themselves. Parents are so accustomed to "being needed" they sometimes miss the declarations of independence that are part of a child's transition into adulthood. Respect their need to do things themselves when they express it. This is important.

THE BIGGIE

Okay, we're going to have to address this. Your primary relationship is going to have to be pretty sturdy for this phase of life—at least if you want things to proceed on a traditional basis. All day every day is a lot of each other. Think about it carefully and talk about what you both need and feel.

Men accustomed to having their wives available 100 percent of the time evenings and weekends are often surprised to find they're not ready for that kind of on-call status 24/7. Everybody needs some alone time, and you each need a life. One of the most frustrating things I observed with my parents was my mother's unwillingness to take classes as a retired person unless my father would enroll as well. Mom had a degree in intellectual history and loved the mental gymnastics of college coursework. Dad had gone to work right out of high school to help support his family after his father died. He was a practical problem solver who learned better in less formal contexts. No way was he going to follow Mom onto a college campus. Mom's insistence that he go for her to be able to go meant she didn't do something that would have brought her a great deal of enjoyment. What a waste.

You may be at a point where you need to decide if you even want a primary relationship. Do you like to do a lot with the same person? Some successful silver singles have different companions for different activities. Dancing with Jeffrey. Golf with George. Hiking with Tony or Paul. An article on single women in *AARP* magazine acknowledged that not all older women want to be married. Further, "Many women are surprised at how learning to be alone, in the best sense of the word, opens them up to a bigger world." This isn't just a "girl" thing. Do *you* want to be married? How do you want this part of your life to work?

Some interesting things happen between men and women at this point. In our younger years, women want to get married. Biology pushes them toward that focus. If they are going to have kids, they need to the stability of marriage so they have the help and resources to raise them.

When we are older, marriage appeals more to men. Study after study supports that men are healthier and stay active longer if they are married. When older women were interviewed by one researcher, one striking commonality was that they tended to see their own lives starting when their marriages ended—for whatever reason.

This is not to say that all men want to be married and all women want to be single. The point to be made is that it's different from when we were young. And that's not all that's different. Women tend to become more assertive and men often become more nurturing as they step into retirement. This is biology—hormones to be exact.

Dr. Christiane Northrup explained it well in *The Wisdom of Menopause*. Both women and men have the hormones estrogen and testosterone in their systems. It's the proportions that make the difference. As women move past their childbearing years, their estrogen levels—which trigger nurturing behaviors—decline. Their testosterone levels—which trigger more assertive behaviors—stay the same. So the proportion moves toward the testosterone end of the balance. Women become more assertive. For men, aging involves a reduction in testosterone. That moves their proportion more toward the estrogen end of the balance. The result is a greater interest in nurturing and support behaviors than before. Women may want to make things happen while men may want to watch or even cheer. The roles are the reverse of what we worked with as young adults.

We need to know this to be able to relate to the opposite sex effectively. Strong older women are ready to start businesses. Strong older men are comfortable changing a grandbaby's diaper.

When I divorced, I assumed I would re-couple within a few years. Two, maybe three max. I am now into that third year and have not come close to wanting to do that. As I learn more about myself, I realize I still have a lot of false information on file about how to be coupled. I also have a huge amount of energy that might be hard for a guy moving toward mellow to be comfortable with every day. For me, being part of a couple is still probably a ways off. I need to learn more about how to use my energy. And until I can get beyond the idea that being part of a traditional couple is like going back to prison, it ain't gonna happen. Trying to force it would be a disservice to both parties.

It's also a disservice to stay in a relationship if your heart is no longer in it. The idea that you should just "tough it out" because "there aren't that many years left" is insane. You may have as much as four decades left together. Staying together and sniping at each other is a form of cruelty. If you are still in love, get counseling. If you aren't, get on with it. Respect, appreciation, and trust are the minimum daily requirements for a primary relationship. For me to to consider coupling again, there's also going to have to be a whole lot of FUN. Life is too short to spend it sleeping next to someone you don't like any more.

The economic ramifications of a choice to split are real. But so are the health ramifications of staying together when you are no longer suited. This is a tough one but an important one. Be honest with yourself and then with your spouse. If you want sex and never get it, something's wrong. If you want to go to Paris on vacation and there's money for that, but you never end up there, there's something wrong. Pretending there isn't will not make it better. The longer you wait to deal with it, the less you will have of the life you want—and deserve—to live.

LENDING A HAND

Quite often, "volunteering" is at the top of the list of things people want to do when they retire. A survey done by Civic Ventures as reported by Rosabeth Moss Kanter found that "a majority of Americans between the ages of 50 and 70 want to benefit their communities by helping the poor, the elderly, and children, or by improving the quality of life through the arts or the environment." Yes, lending a hand is a good idea. But don't go into it clueless.

Knowing yourself is every bit as important in this context as in the rest of what we've been talking about. Volunteer situations vary extensively. Knowing what you need from your volunteer activities can make a huge difference in both your satisfaction with the commitment and with your effectiveness as part of the effort. Knowing how well your personality and priorities fit with the organization's needs is the first piece of a good volunteer effort.

A few years ago, I worked as a volunteer gardener at a botanical garden here in the Pacific Northwest. I signed on in *November*. I wanted to do some sort of volunteer effort that was outdoors and related to plants. I thought I had it all figured out. That time around, I got MORE than what I thought I needed. I worked in the wet and the cold, but with very warm people beside me. I learned a lot about how to garden in the Pacific Northwest, but also had the solitude to discover some of the beautiful parallels between physical gardening and honoring the Divine. It was a very well run program. From day one, I was ready to just be a worker. Much as I tend to end up leading, often by default, that was not the case in this context. They had good leaders. I just showed up and did what they told me to. It was exactly what I wanted and needed.

In contrast, after Hurricane Katrina hit, I got "serious" about volunteering and joined the Red Cross. They said they needed leaders to relieve those who'd already been there three weeks. I am a leader. I thought they meant me. I pushed through all the required training as fast as I could and in five weeks was deployed to Texas in the aftermath of Hurricane Rita. This time it was different. I was plunked in the middle of the chaos of a natural disaster under leadership that could, at best, be described as benevolent incompetence. By that point, the Red Cross *was* the disaster. The need to lead pulled inside me like a sled dog ready to run. My ability to get things done should have been priceless with all that needed to be accomplished. Instead, it was useless. Well, worse than useless. Being in the chaos and powerless to improve it was excruciating.

The Red Cross is an organization with over a century of tradition that defines its personality. It runs on seniority. Much as they had begged for more "leadership" volunteers, the organization was unable to use them when they arrived because they didn't come with previous years of service to the Red Cross. That was the only way the Red Cross defined competence.

If you'd been there 20 years, you were good. If you'd only been with them a month or two, it was a given that you didn't know anything. There was so much we could have done better if there had been a way for them to understand what we knew *before* we signed on with the Red Cross.

The Red Cross isn't the only outfit that has trouble with this challenge. Knowing how to use volunteers well is a lot harder than using employees well—and even that isn't done effectively a lot of the time. Much as it's a problem that needs to be addressed, it has not been yet. You need to know that. Take a good, long, well-informed look at where you want to volunteer. Are they going to let you use the skills, ability, talent, and experience you have to offer right away? Are you willing to hang around long enough for them to decide you do know something? I'm not suggesting you not volunteer. Just know what you're getting into.

You can take at least two other routes that avoid this dilemma. If you've been involved with the organization for years, it's a moot point. They already know what you can do. There may even be some carryover with a national organization if you decide to move to a different part of the country once you retire. Or not.

The other solution is to volunteer in situations that involve smaller, less organizationally stiff groups or to do things one-on-one. Last weekend, I hiked with a third grade teacher who was frustrated with the amount of help one of her students needed. The little girl had both mental and physical challenges plus an unsupportive home environment. My teacher friend's choices were to either focus on the struggling student to the detriment of the other 21 kids in the class or to give the other kids what they needed and let the little girl fall behind.

The answer, of course, is a volunteer who is willing to work with the little girl one-on-one. But the teacher doesn't have the network or time to find that person. Looking for that kind of opportunity when you have time to volunteer might be a better fit for you than taking the hundreds of hours of additional training that an outfit like the Red Cross needs before they will accept you as "qualified."

The variety of volunteer opportunities is endless. One friend just got back from building a composting latrine for the families whose livelihood comes from gleaning the dump in Mexico City. Another spends her Tuesday afternoons handing out food at her church's food bank. My up the hill neighbor rocks babies at a local hospital. A few years ago, I helped non-English speaking clients of the local literacy council write resumes for their job searches. You can build trails. You can spearhead establishing a Boys & Girls Club in your community. Choose well. It should be fun for you as well as service. You will only stick with these things if they strike a cord for you—if they are satisfying.

There's a concept in Eastern philosophy I learned as "equal energy exchange." It's particularly useful in considering volunteer opportunities. The premise is that for things to continue in any situation, there has to be equivalence between the value of what is being given and that being received *by each person involved*. The equivalence is not measured in identical units though. For example, I pay someone to cut my hair. She gives me confidence from having a good haircut; I give her the money to pay her bills. If how she cuts my hair doesn't give me that confidence, the balance is gone and I won't do that anymore. If I don't pay her enough, the balance is gone for her and she won't let me make an appointment again. Likewise if part of why I volunteer is to use my competencies, I'm not going to stay if all I get to do is stuff envelopes.

In the volunteer context, the equivalence will most likely involve some kind of emotional pay off for the person volunteering. Maybe the organization makes you feel appreciated for what you do. Maybe there is a sense of belonging that makes you feel good about doing it. Maybe you get jazzed by the difference you make in the lives of those you help. The thing to remember is, despite the need to "give back" that we tend to feel more acutely as we get older, there has to be something in it for you for a volunteer effort to work. It won't be paid in dollars, but it needs to be there for you to be able to stick with it. So know what you want to get out of the experience as well as what you want to give.

Think ✎ and Do

Knowing your emotions is hard until you start paying attention to them. But emotions hold the keys to some of the sweetest, most meaningful moments in your life. Can you identify how you feel about the important things? Do you know when a surface answer isn't enough and are you willing to dig deeper on those? Do you claim your emotions? Do you accept them or blame someone else for "causing" them? Most key, do you know enough to help yourself move from emotions that hold you down to emotions that empower you?

Exercise 6.1—PINCH POINTS

Rate each of the following statements using a number from 1 to 9. "1" means the statement is not at all true for you. "9" means it describes you perfectly. Circle the N/A if the statement doesn't apply for your situation.

RATING VALUES

Not at all like me: 1 2 3 4 5 6 7 8 9 : Totally me

My spouse/partner is awesome. N/A				
I do things I'm afraid to do.				
Young people today don't care about anyone else.				
I want to give back to my community.				
I like my situation regarding a life partner.				
My fears are about real dangers.				
When you get to age 60, the fun is pretty much gone.				
This time of my life is about making a difference.				
I respect my spouse/partner immensely. N/A				
I use fear as a motivator for myself.				
I hate the idea of being "old".				

There's got to be a way for me to help.				
My favorite times are with my spouse/partner. N/A				
When I'm afraid, I find a way to do it anyway.				
Everybody's just out to make money these days—no one cares.				
I'm excited about having time to get involved in charity work.				
I'd trust my spouse/partner with my life. N/A				
I think a little fear makes you perform better.				
The world is in awful shape and it's getting worse.				
I plan to be a positive influence with what I do next.				
TOTALS: Total the numbers in each column. The highest possible score for a column is 45. The lowest is 5 unless you marked any or all as "N/A" scores in Column One. That will make that score lower, perhaps even 1. The column totals are useful only to help you get a sense of yourself. They are not absolute or meant to define what's "correct."				

The first column deals with your satisfaction with your primary relationship. If this score is high, you're probably on solid ground with this part of your life. The numbers are just a way to make you think about these aspects. If you answered automatically, go back and look at each item in the first column again. Did you answer them honestly or are your answers what you want to be there but aren't? If you are not currently in a relationship, are you happy with that situation? If not, what do you want in a relationship as you step into the freedom of retirement? How are you going to go about getting it?

The second column deals with how you relate to fear. A high score means you use it to motivate you to do new things. A low score suggests it may be keeping you from things you really want to do. You may want to shore up your courage and, as Eleanor Roosevelt recommends, "Do the thing you think you cannot do."

The third column deals with negativity. If this score is high, you're buying in on a negative outlook on life. You can do that, but it's not much fun. You may want to explore why you've chosen that attitude and outline steps to move to a more positive vantage so you can enjoy life more.

The fourth column is about giving to your community once you have time. You don't have to do that for your life to be worthwhile, but those who express a desire to do this will be happier if those kinds of opportunities are included. If your score was low, give some thought to what you do want to do with your time. Is it all about leisure? Going back to school? Taking care of relatives who need some help? Sometimes the giving is at the family and friends level rather than for the community. Sometimes giving isn't what it's about at all. But there is usually some component of this (making a difference or having an impact) in what people dream of doing.

Exercise 6.2—LIES OR TRUTH?

Okay, for grins, here's one in the format we all used to love in school (because there's a 50/50 chance you are going to get it right regardless of how much you studied).

	True	False
1. Old people are happy sitting around doing nothing.	___	___
2. Work is for the fools who can't retire.	___	___
3. Younger workers need to just work and stop whining.	___	___
4. Anger is my prerogative.	___	___
5. Doing nothing is good for you.	___	___
6. If something makes you afraid, don't do it.	___	___
7. Never tell anyone about what you want to do.	___	___
8. You should always do what your adult kids need.	___	___
9. "Feeling old" is a normal part of being 60 or more.	___	___
10. A bad childhood means you're scarred for life.	___	___

I do hope you marked every single one of these false. They're all baloney.

Exercise 6.3—TRY THE SHOES

*It's hard to sense your own emotions when you are first trying
to learn how. We're pushed to ignore them from the time we are
in junior high. Below are some situations that typically evoke emotion.
Try to identify what you felt if you've had this experience,
or might feel if you haven't, in each of these situations.*

You hear the first cry of your newborn child or grandchild: _____

_____

Your pet gets in an accident: _____

_____

You see the first crocus after a long, hard, cold winter: _____

_____

A friend tells you something "as a friend" that you didn't want to know:

_____

The highway patrol pulls you over for speeding: _____

_____

Exercise 6.4—YOUR OWN SHOES

*Now look for some recent events that had a strong
emotional component for you.*

My most joyful experience this week: _____

_____

It made me happy because: _____

_____

The saddest thing that happened to me this week: _____

_____

It made me sad because: _____

_____

The most frustrating thing I am dealing with right now: _____

_____

It's frustrating because: _____

_____

The thing that made me really mad most recently: _____

_____

It made me mad because: _____

_____

_____

Icicles and Prickly Things in the Dark

I finally started to accept I had feelings after I forgot how to walk. That was back when I had a baby and a four-year old and no sense of how to take care of myself while I was taking care of them. Something went wrong with medication the doctor prescribed and I ended up in the hospital, "ataxic." I couldn't walk. Literally. After about 10 days, they decided there was nothing wrong with me physically. So they suggested it was in my head. Not exactly. It was in my heart. I was ignoring my own needs to the point my body gave up in protest.

So I went to see a shrink and came away thinking, "Hell, I can do that." I enrolled in graduate school in psychology and started reading. Before it was time to start attending classes, I devoured pop psych books. This was when Dr. Wayne Dyer's *Your Erroneous Zones* had just hit the market. I soaked it up like a sponge after a trip across the Sahara. People actually had a right to feel. And a lot of what you felt depended on what you were telling yourself. The power of learning that was awesome. Old hat, you may be saying. It was like quark theory for me. I could not get enough. I read and read and read. I was awake again.

I wish I could report that this was all there was to it, but sometimes I am a very slow learner. The introduction to the concepts in the 70's made it to my brain. I still had a long way to go before they resided in my heart. Which meant I had even farther to go to give myself that unavoidable essential, the right to feel whatever I was feeling.

Instead, I went from not feeling at all to feeling what was fashionable to feel. I was liberated. I was "open and honest." I was ready to take on every bad thing that ever happened in my life and hold those who'd "been responsible" accountable. It's probably just as well that I ran out of time as the kids got into school and sports and I got deeper into my graduate studies. I was on the wrong road, so pulling off and parking the feeling thing for a while wasn't any worse than what I was doing.

Then I got the chance to go to work. Woo hoo! I was now a legitimate part of society. I was also too busy to notice I wasn't paying any attention to what I was feeling again.

I ended up divorced—the "in" solution to marital problems at the time. Now I was a single mom and full time executive. Feelings? I welled with love when I looked at my sleeping children. I breathed a sigh of relief when I realized I was quite able to pay the bills on my own. But there was still no internal conversation about what I needed, wanted, hoped, feared, or loathed.

Cue "The Second Time Around." I fell in love with someone who seemed perfect. I moved myself and my sons 600 miles to marry him. I was in love—and that is definitely a heady feeling. But was I paying attention to my own needs? No, not yet.

In less than a year I'd developed fibroid tumors and was told I needed a hysterectomy. What I really needed was a divorce. The "perfect man" was a cold abuser—the kind of guy who has no problem at all convincing you that you aren't feeling what you're feeling. A guy who was certain that if everything was fine for him, I didn't have a problem.

I held this pain silently at first, mortified and terrified that I'd made such a horrendous mistake. I convinced myself I just needed to find the right way to talk to him and then everything would be fine. Classic words of an abused spouse even if the bruises were on my psyche and not my arms. But I didn't know what was going on was abuse. I was sure that if I could make him understand, he would be nice to me.

It wasn't until I'd left the corporate world and moved to the Pacific Northwest that I began to aggressively work on defining what I needed in my own life to be happy. I was 55 before I started to act consistently in my own best interest.

Let's not pretend this was all dank and dark. And I am certainly not suggesting it was "all his fault." I willingly lived this life. In the obvious ways, it was comfortable. I planned fun for others, and I had fun myself. But there was a hollowness that persisted that brought me to thoughts of "why bother?" way too often.

It took my dad's death to push me into action. Maybe he was giving me his strength from the beyond. I moved out and insisted that things change. My then husband said they would so I moved back in. I still believed it was just a matter of getting him to understand. Things stopped changing as soon as I returned home. I insisted, and he resisted. I doubt he knew what he was doing, but even when I told him what was hurting me, I got more of the same. "How can you not be happy? Everything is working great." When I finally got through to him that it was not "great" for me, he blamed me—complaining I didn't know how to be happy and that nothing he did was ever right. That, too, is a classic strategy for a cold abuser: Make the person think she really doesn't know what's going on. I had to fight really hard to stop believing I was the one who wasn't doing what was needed to make the relationship work.

THEN I started to look at what I needed. Sincerely. Without limits. I was finally to the point that if I'd decided I needed to join the Peace Corps, I would. If I needed to start playing tuba, I was ready to find someone to give me lessons.

What I needed was to dance. Without an icicle partner. Fully alive as myself. Alone—but with others in the same space. I discovered a group doing transformative dance once a week. It's a physical/spiritual practice where you dance you own dance to a broad range of music in ways that come close to, and sometimes go beyond, prayer.

Movement in that context helped me find what I felt. Releasing the tension in my physical muscles left room to release the yearnings and pain I'd held tight inside for so long. It wasn't just my *right* to be me and my *right* to seek means of meeting my own needs. I finally understood that it's a *responsibility*. You can't do much good if you don't know what you came to do. The roadmap for what you came to do resides in your heart. The only way to access it is by paying attention to what you need.

The idea that meeting my own needs is service to the greater good blew my mind. It still does sometimes. The power of being authentic can be awesome. When I'm true to myself, things I need fall into place. When I lose track and start down someone else's path, my good fortune and ease dry up—sometimes instantly. Now, if I start to sense something isn't going well, that's the first thing I check: Am I doing what I really want to do here? Am I meeting my commitment to myself with how I am spending my time and energy?

If you stay focused on what you need and want, you can make the needed alterations easily. They are small course corrections not monumental diversions when handled on an ongoing basis. I did not do small course corrections. I overhauled my whole life. It took a huge amount of work, a boatload of courage, and more trust and patience than I ever thought I would need in my entire life.

Being authentic involves being graceful. It's not necessary to brutalize others to get what you need. Legitimate needs are not zero-sum situations. True needs have a calm about them that's curative in itself. Anger isn't part of it, even if someone is yelling in your face. There's a quiet, confident focus that comes from knowing yourself that makes you feel eight feet tall. You can do it. You will do it. It will all happen the way it's supposed to. Really.

Focus. Wait. Act when you see the next thing. And don't assume you already know what that "next thing" is.

That brings up the last aspect of meeting your needs. Stay open. I'm too embarrassed to count the number of times I've wanted a certain thing to get me going in a direction I perceived I needed to go—a job, a writing contract, even a date. When it actually arrives, it usually doesn't look like what I've prescribed at all. It's usually a lot better.

Stay open to whatever comes.

Openness helps so much in the quest to understand yourself. Your heart is where the treasure map resides. But what you *think* is in your heart and what is really there are going to be different sometimes. Accept that. Know it is part of the journey.

Give yourself permission to feel your feelings. Emotional honesty is a super highway through the territory of You. Get comfortable driving that road. It will take you to riches beyond measure.

Chapter Seven:

Managing Zucchini

It's August, and my garden runneth over—with zucchini. Last night I made three loaves of zucchini bread. At least I intend to use those. A week ago, I made one loaf of a new version, tasted it, and threw it out. I'll do my part, but enough is enough.

This time of year, I pore through the "z" section of a lot of cookbooks. Did you know there's a recipe for zucchini *pie?* This is a real dessert that takes a cup and half of sugar. Haven't tried that, but I do put zucchini in casseroles. I put it in salads. Frittata? Torte? I might even sneak it into chili if it gets cool enough to make some. Maybe we could get Jones to add it as a flavor in their soda line.

The bounty of zucchini is legendary. So is the gardener's tendency to accept its fecundity as a personal responsibility. I give it away whenever I can. But there's always "more." I've cured myself of the Use It Up game, but I am still way too devoted to managing my zucchini.

Why have I been toiling for Zucchini Rescue? The hole in the ozone won't widen if I don't use every single little green squash. Still, it's become my life in the last few weeks.

This is often how our day-to-day priorities end up getting set—by the zucchini in our lives. We never stop to assess whether we really *need* to be worrying about whatever it is we're in the middle of because we're spending all our time dealing with it. Purpose gets lost in the name of immediate problem solving. Aim gets erased with instant action. Meaning falls prey to the squeaky wheel.

It's not zucchini we're talking about here. It's everything. The stuff we acquire. The responsibilities we take on. The work we've been doing for decades. The friends who just show up and keep asking for things—or suggesting ways to spend time you don't really have. It becomes zucchini when it is running us instead of the reverse.

When we're doing it because it's there to do—not because it's a high priority for us personally—it's often accompanied by a certain level of restlessness. "There's got to be more than this" and "I know I'm here to do *something* meaningful and *this isn't it*" are common refrains. We do the work, but it's not a source of satisfaction. We do the work, and it drains us. And then we tell ourselves we're tired because we're "getting old." Arghhhh!

When sense of purpose and use of time are inconsistent, you're gonna be tired. Period. End of sentence. Age is not the issue. Meaning is.

This chapter is about the spiritual level of our lives—where purpose is born and raised and lives forever. The level that's so easy to lose track of in the hustle and bustle of raising a family, earning a wage, living the day-to-day life. *Meaning is the part that makes the rest work well.* And work well enough that we are having fun at it even when it demands way more than we think we have to give. The part that gets us jazzed.

Please don't tell me you know Jesus and assume you have it covered because you're involved in a church. If your church serves you, of course you want to be involved. But you are still responsible for keeping purpose and performance synchronized. I've watched way too many people go to church on Sunday and even say all the right words all week and then DO something entirely different. I don't want to talk about religion here. I want to talk about soul. About the fire at the center of the center of your belly.

About passion

What are you *passionate* about? You might read that question, give a weary sigh, and mutter, "I don't have time for passion." Those who don't have time to get real are the same folks we'll meet at the emergency room in the middle of a heart attack or in court in the middle of a divorce they didn't see coming. When we pay attention only to the things that *demand* it, we're physically still here, but we're spiritually dead. We are not fun to be around when that happens—not even for ourselves.

The word "passion" has become distressingly passé though. Pop psych has owned it for too long. Passion is an ordinary word, and it belongs to ordinary people. What makes your heart sing? What makes you think you just climbed Everest when you finish it?

I was startled to find a piece of my own passion in a meeting a few months back. Five of us were working on plans for the first phase of a community-wide public art planning project. There we were, five intelligent, diverse women gathered around my dining room table, batting around ideas. Hammering out what would work best for a project that went way beyond us. At a particularly collaborative moment, I realized I was *immensely* jazzed by what we were doing. What was even more surprising was, though the content area was worthy, it was the process that had me stoked. I love to solve problems in a group. I'd not been aware enough of myself to realize it's part of my passion until that day.

Passion can be pretty elusive if you have the conventional version of a life. It's not a one-size fits all thing you can pick up on your next errand run. In fact, I can't even help you uncover it with this book if you are simply reading the words. Passion demands action. *Finding* your passion also demands action. You have to look for it. It's not going to walk up and introduce itself.

Where do you find passion? Unless you were born to be a buyer for the store, it's not at Nordstrom. Safeway isn't going to stock it either. This is sounding like a broken record, but finding your passion is just like finding the rest of you. You have to figure out who you are. Once you start to do the work, the information arrives in the most unexpected ways. But you have to do the work. Really. Please believe me about this. I've spent quite a few years trying to avoid that work with frustrating results. So let me say it again. If you want to live a satisfying life, you need to understand what satisfies you. *Get to know yourself.*

And the most important things to know reside at the spiritual level. What are your values? What do you really believe about why you are here? About why *anybody* is here? How does a good life work? What's in it? What's not?

For most of my life, I've felt if you lined everyone in the world up according to what they really believed instead of by the religion they professed, the people who ended up together wouldn't be of the same faith. For a while I was cynic enough to think there was something wrong with this. There isn't. Faith and personal philosophy are not prescribed. They are acquired experience by experience. Since each of us collects a unique set of experiences, the philosophy that results is going to be one of a kind. Yes, there will be similarities for many of us, but we are not identical in what we choose to believe. So...you may be a Catholic or a Muslim or an elder in the Church of the Latter-day Saints. You are still unique. Cherish that.

VALUES

Harkness provides a 70-item inventory of common values in her book *Don't Stop the Career Clock*. She advises people to choose their top 10. Her list has a career orientation because it was designed to help assess values *on the job*. There's more to it than that, but the list is a good start toward thinking in terms of values in general. Of even greater value is her "glass balls/rubber balls" analogy. Our deepest values are like glass balls—we never want to drop them. Lesser values are rubber balls—we may lose hold of them—or chose to drop them—without dire consequences. Only you can identify which is which for you. Only you can identify what you value at all.

The Artist's Way, Julia Cameron's incredible 12-week course book for everyone—not just artists, provides processes for going a bit deeper than that. Use both, use either, use neither, but use something. *What is most important to you?*

I value honesty. Authenticity. Sincerity. Commitment. Connection. Caring. These are my glass balls, and they don't change. Some others weave in and out. Sometimes creativity is a high priority; sometimes mental acuity is. Sometimes organization is at the top of the list, and sometimes chaos is okay. It's still the same set, I'm just not using all of them all the time. But when I was working from external cues, the values expressed in whatever I was doing were inconsistent. When my response came from that set of cues, it was sometimes the total opposite of where I actually stood personally. That is an ineffective way to live, believe me. It's hard to create a strong sense of self from someone else's values. Get to know your own. Stand on your own bedrock.

My position on rules is an example of this. For the first 50 years of my life, I thought I was a rule *follower*. That came from my need to be a "good girl" in the eyes of those I was trying to please. I actually dislike rules. I tend to operate best at the leading edge—on the frontier. In that context, rules made for existing situations are often irrelevant or worse.

JUDGMENT

Okay. Any of you balk at one or more of the things I said were important to me? It's okay. We've been at this for a while—we're friends by now. I did it myself—when I got to commitment. That's a toughie for me. Why would I value that given the mess I've made of things by putting it in the wrong places? It's still part of me though. It's very important to me to keep my word. When I don't follow through on even a small thing, it bothers me more than a hundred mosquito bites.

The point here isn't about what I value. It's about that reaction. Judgment. There are times when we *must* judge but also times when doing so gives us less than we can have. As Dr. Jim Dreaver puts it in *The*

Ultimate Cure, "...judgment in terms of making wise choices and decisions is healthy. But to be judgmental in the sense of putting yourself and others down...closes down your heart....Getting free of judgment is an essential step to freedom."

Every time you decide how someone else *should* be, you've wasted a chance to connect. You've wasted a chance to accept. You wasted a chance to raft the river of life and instead took a powerboat up the dead-end slough of control. We lose so much time and energy trying to make other people be like us. What do we gain with that?

We gain the comfort of familiarity if we can actually pull it off. But we lose the chance to learn things and to experience a broader life than we can have "among our own." There would be peace on earth if we could just learn to let each other be who we are. But that requires not judging others by our own values. And that's hard.

Right now, I'm living in a small suburban city in the Pacific Northwest. I'm not sure how much longer that will be the case. There is a provincialism here that surprises and bothers me. Many in my community take great pride in having lived 40, 50, 90 years in this same place. I do not value that. I'm a pioneer. I need to move on when things get too familiar. So, as long as I live here, I will struggle to not judge the ones who believe in staying put.

COMPASSION AND SURRENDER

"Compassion," if you come at it from the Latin root words, means "to bear or suffer with." Webster contends it means "sympathetic consciousness of others' distress together with a desire to alleviate it." In *Walking Between the Worlds: The Science of Compassion*, Greg Braden takes it way beyond a noun and delineates it as a way of life. He defines compassion as a combination at three different levels: "*Thought* without attachment to the event. *Emotion* without the charge of polarity. *Feeling* without the distortion of bias and conditions."

Compassion, in this sense, is the ability to see what is going on without deciding if it's "bad" or "good" and without getting wrapped up in it emotionally. This is a tall order, but life becomes incredibly sweet for me when I can manage to live that way. The Buddhists call it detachment. We could also call it letting go. Surrender.

Unfortunately for most of us, the word surrender itself creates angst. *Surrender* implies defeat at the tribal level. Wars end in conquest and victory or surrender and defeat—or annihilation. Surrender in that sense is disgrace. At the community level, surrender implies inferiority and failure.

Surrender at the spiritual level is a whole different thing. What we surrender spiritually is our separateness. We give up the idea we are alone—that others must be exactly like us for us to able to connect with them. And the impossibility of connecting because "No one is like me." With that thinking, there is no one to turn to. We are not part of anything larger than ourselves. We have to make it work exclusively on our own.

That's a way of life most of us end up living by default. You look like you're alone when you stand in front of the mirror. You seem pretty much alone when you are wolfing down cold cereal for dinner at the kitchen counter. That aloneness is an illusion we choose. That aloneness is what we need to surrender.

The thing we need to get past is how "silly" it seems to believe there IS more. Believing we are part of something larger is a choice, nothing more, nothing less. Call it "the Force" or God or Jahweh…the Universe…the Divine. You choose the title and you choose the way you want to view that power. This is the ultimate choice actually. The rest of your life will be colored by how you see this key aspect.

A recent literature review reported that 85 to 90 percent of Americans say they believe in God. The study goes on to note "under the surface, American religion is startlingly complex and diverse." I would hope so.

You will never find the science to back up whatever you decide to believe. Disproving the null hypothesis is not an option. You'll never be able to point to facts to support it. But science and facts are not the only tools to use in making choices. This one is better done using your gut—and your heart.

The choice you decide to own about the nature of the Divine is not something you need to announce to the world if that makes you uncomfortable. Please be aware that some of those you care about might notice though. Embracing your own truth here might be alarming to some of them. There are a lot of folks taking external direction on this from organized religion. If that works for them, well and good. But the choice of what works for you is YOURS.

Even if you don't have that kind of pressure, there might be folks who react negatively to your choice to see yourself as part of all there is. Separate people can be needy people. If your circle expects you to be needy and you start coming in calm and together, it's gonna bother at least some of them. Separate people can also be willing to carry way more than their share of the load—as a way to soothe the ache of isolation. People who have been reaping the benefit of that kind of effort might not give it up graciously.

Make no mistake, these choices are big ones. They are also the ones that get you on track fastest. You can muck around for months trying to get clear on whether you want to work part time for a CPA or start your own business when you retire and then make a whole different choice in a second once you surrender to the idea the Universe has something in mind.

I am not suggesting surrender to some cult, or even to a specific religion. I am recommending surrender to the idea you really are here to do something and the Universe is with you on that. Spiritual surrender is about *connection*—about tapping into a force much larger than yourself. Tony Schwartz nails it in his introduction in *What Really Matters*. Describing his own situation as a young, successful author, he says, "...somehow it hadn't translated into a sense of depth, or richness, or passion in my life... What I longed for was to feel more at home with myself, more deeply comfortable in my own skin, more connected to something timeless and essential, more real." He spent the next four years seeking out and learning from people who "made the search for meaning primary in their lives."

Spiritual surrender is the start of something really big. I wish there was an easy way to convince you of that. At the tribal level surrender implies a total loss of power. The reverse is true at the spiritual level. "Surrender to the Divine" means you are connected to all the power that is.

Surrender involves trust. Trust requires courage. Courage is when you do what you need to even when you are scared to death of doing it. Trust will never be part of a "safe" life. Whenever you trust, you take a risk. But there are risks when you don't trust, too. In *I Could Do Anything if I Only Knew What It Was*, Barbara Sher warns "When you play it too safe, *you are taking the biggest risk of your life*." The truth of that is even more compelling in this context. Playing it safe here means you continue to isolate yourself. Stop assuming it's you against the world and that you are alone in the battle. Life is more profound when you accept you are part of something bigger.

Sacred Contracts

When you start to see the world as interconnected, everything has a purpose. The nail that flattened your left rear tire, the bee that chased you out of the garden, your lunch. I met this concept and its ramifications in the book *Sacred Contracts* by Caroline Myss. Nothing I do has been the same since.

Throughout my youth and during much of my adult life I have dutifully recited a meal prayer that went "BlessusohLordandtheseThygiftswhichweareabouttoreceivefromThybountythroughChristourLordAmen." That's the way we always said it—in a single breath, without stopping at the end of the words. One mega-multi-syllabic word. Now I look at the food and thank whoever gave so that I have it.

Lots of times, this does not involve words. But it is a three-times-a-day reminder of sacred contracts. When I realize something (animal or plant) *had* to die so I could eat, I am grateful that's what it came to do with its life. *Being my food* was that thing's purpose. I want to do right by it—by all the stuff I eat to survive. They all gave the ultimate so I could thrive. I need to do my best to use that food wisely and well—to use that nutrition for the highest and best good.

Okay, maybe I'm getting a bit too intense. But there's a reason to bring it up. We're each part of that same effort. What we do makes something else possible. When we do the thing we came to do—when we focus our lives on the things we love—on what gives us meaning—we make a difference. Because it is then we are honoring our sacred contracts.

As the Persian poet Rumi exhorted, "Let yourself be drawn by the strange pull of what you really love. It will not lead you astray." It will not lead you astray because it is the Universe connecting you to what you came to do. It will guide you with the bright light of meaning.

"Significant Quality"

Bear with me; I need to hit Webster's one more time. Beyond the context of the language itself, "meaning" is defined as "significant quality." Meaning in life means what you are doing makes you feel worthwhile. Like showing up was worth the effort.

In this age of "here, I know what you need," meaning is a major challenge. An organized religion will expect you to find meaning in its agenda. A car company will want you to find meaning in its newest model. Friends might want you to find meaning in helping them move. These are all potentially worthy parts of your life. But they will not satisfy you for long if you simply take what other people offer. You have to find your own meaning. I'm sure you're getting sick of hearing that. But it's the only way to make this work.

At one point in this convoluted process I call a career path, a dear and wise friend suggested I get into mediation. She had some compelling arguments to back the idea up. She noted (accurately) that I love to solve problems. I like to work with people. I'm good at coming up with creative solutions and finding unusual ways to get the impossible done. Perfect! I went roaring off to volunteer convinced I'd found my new career niche. I had it all planned before I even showed up for the first session: I would work with the mediation center, take the training, and become a professional. I'd be seeing clients on a paying basis in less than a year.

I wasn't quite to the point of printing business cards before reality set in. Yes, on the surface this sounded like an excellent match of skills and profession. I was good at the things a mediator needs to be good at. But after a few hours of talking to distraught people about how to resolve things they were fighting about with other people— particularly spouses in the process of divorce—I threw in the towel.

What was I thinking? I was in the middle of highly stressful marital situation myself. I didn't need anyone else's marital woes to deal with. My own were plenty. I needed to be of service. I needed to help. Just not that way. That level of information had to come from inside me though. My friend saw me as competent. She's right—I ooze competence. What she couldn't see was the magnitude of what I was dealing with emotionally at the time.

Meaning. Meaningful work. Meaningful relationships. A meaningful life. Meaning full. This is the pith of it. If you can identify what gives your life meaning, the rest will fall into place as you honor it.

There is, at least if my own route is any indication, at lot of room for wrong turns and unplanned detours in the process though. I did two years of "not me" before I got to where I am now. I "tried on" option and after option hoping to find what I was supposed to do next. With each "next thing" I started out enthralled with the answer. Each time, I believed I'd finally found it. It was excruciating to end up at "not me" again and again. I hated it. I have been decisive my entire life—I can point to compelling examples from elementary school. This inability to decide made me wonder if I was losing my mind.

Now, I can see I had to live that. I had to be able to report on it for you. I had to do it so I could get past it and then wave on those who might be stuck in the same swamp. Keep going. It ends. You will find solid ground and be able to take good strong strides again eventually, even if you are so bogged down right now that it takes days to get one foot pulled from the mud.

Take the risk. Reach out. Connect to the Universe and to other people. Trust you really are here for a reason. Then pay attention to what excites you as you try new things, to what stirs your soul as you sift through the possibilities that present themselves.

You are here. Be grateful and do something good.

Think and Do

The spiritual aspects of a life surface more easily after we have some experience. Our personal philosophies evolve as a way of making sense of what happens to us. So as we get to retirement age, we have a much broader, more complete manual to work from. Accessing it may be a matter of course for you. If not, now is the time to work on that. Being able to express what's at the center of your soul makes it easier to make choices that are consistent with that belief system.

Below are some exercises to help you get to that level of proficiency. Please note, this is a high marshmallow area. You need to be able to verbalize these for *yourself.* You're going to get really stale spiritually if you keep this stuff out and pass it around all the time. This is your deepest truth. Share it only with people who will respect it.

Exercise 7.1—THIS I BELIEVE

Essay test! Use the space below—or better yet, grab a sheet of paper or a big fat yellow pad. Write all you can about what you believe at the deepest level—the meaning of life, how/if God (or whatever name you want) fits in, what role humans play and you play in particular, etc. Include anything that comes to mind and keep writing as long as you can.

_____
_____
_____
_____
_____
_____

Taking the time to think about what you believe instead of just giving yourself a religion label can clear away a lot of the debris hiding the meaning you seek for your life. There is no easy way to do this. Well, this IS the easy way. It beats 10 years of therapy or two at an ashram somewhere in India.

Exercise 7.2—THE OPINIONS OF OTHERS

Here are 10 sayings often quoted as part of how to live a good life. Record your initial reaction when you read them. Is that reaction at odds what you want to say you believe after you think about it?

1. No good deed goes unpunished.

Reaction: _____
_____
_____

Reaction to the reaction: _____
_____
_____

2. He who has the money has the power.

Reaction:_____
_____
_____

Reaction to the reaction: _____

_____

_____

3. Everything happens the way it's supposed to.

Reaction: _____

_____

_____

Reaction to the reaction: _____

_____

_____

4. Many hands make light work.

Reaction: _____

_____

_____

Reaction to the reaction: _____

_____

_____

5. He who hesitates is lost.

Reaction: _____

_____

_____

Reaction to the reaction: _____

_____

_____

6. Cowards die a thousand times; the valiant never taste of death but once.

Reaction: _____

_____

_____

Reaction to the reaction: _____

_____

_____

7. A fool and his money are soon parted.

Reaction: _____

_____

_____

Reaction to the reaction: _____

_____

_____

8. It's not the size of the dog in the fight; it's the size of the fight in the dog.

Reaction: _____

_____

_____

Reaction to the reaction: _____

_____

_____

9. Never attribute to malice what can be explained by ignorance.

Reaction: _____

_____

_____

Reaction to the reaction: _____

_____

_____

10. **Fall down seven times, stand up eight.**

Reaction: _____

_____

_____

Reaction to the reaction: _____

_____

_____

Exercise 7.3—SACRED CONTRACTS

Let's start small in terms of seeing the connectedness of Sacred Contracts. Give your assessment of the purpose of the existence of each of these things. (Hopefully all things you are not personally attached to.)

An amusement park ride

Purpose: _____

_____

A clothesline

Purpose: _____

_____

Angelina Jolie

Purpose: _____

_____

A sports team

Purpose: _____

_____

An impossible relative

Purpose: _____

_____

I'll give you what I came up with as a first pass, just to get you in the groove. If you don't feel you have it down, go back through and try it again, or come up with five of your own.

- *Amusement park ride*: There to help people have fun, relax and forget their worries; to provide employment to the person running the ride; to provide a livelihood to those who've invested money in the ride company's stock or revenue to the bank that loaned them money to buy the ride.

- *Clothesline*: To provide a place for clothes to dry in the natural air; to provide the "center line" for a kids' tent made with a bed sheet; to tie down a load that's going to the dump in the family pickup; to tie up a wayward animal (Horse? Llama? Camel?)

- *Angelina Jolie*: To help people relax by watching a movie she's acted in; to bring to light humanitarian problems in Third World countries; to provide the tabloids and popular magazines with something to write about.

- *Sports Team*: To entertain the fans with games; to employ the members of the team; to create scandals that sell newspapers.

- *Impossible Relative*: To teach other family members patience, tolerance, and coping strategies; to serve as an example of what you *don't* want to be; to create a situation that requires the family to learn how to problem solve together.

The gist of your own contracts is likely to be on a much different scale than these. However, thinking this way, even in such everyday kinds of contexts, changes how you react in situations.

In *Anatomy of the Spirit*, Caroline Myss advocates taking the time to define your Code of Honor. The power within that process is pretty amazing. A code of honor reflects your values, your purpose, and your sense of how the world works. It doesn't have to be an elaborate effort.

Exercise 7.4—CODE OF HONOR

Write out your code of honor. These are the premises that define how you are going to live you life. What "rules" make it all make sense for you?

_____

_____

_____

_____

_____

_____

_____

_____

_____

_____

_____

_____

_____

_____

When I first did this exercise, I was using the backside of writing drafts—torn in quarters for even more mileage. I wrote my Code of Honor on those—more than once. For a while, I wrote a new one every few days, just to see if it would be any different. It wasn't then. But I just did it again recently. The longer term demonstrates some big differences. I value learning and growth, so that's good news for me.

Here's a version I wrote five years ago:

- I act based on what's true for me. I listen to my heart and my wisdom in making decisions.

- My aloneness is therapeutic and necessary.

- Creating is the source of my power. I *must* write.

- I have what I need to do what I came to do as part of God.

- I make each day sacred and fill them with conscious living.

- I forgive all trespasses and seek to heal any I have caused.

Here's what it looked like the last time I did it—a couple months ago.

RULES FOR THE NEXT DECADE

1. Include guys. (But don't worship them.)
2. Laugh a lot.
3. Love, nurture, and support your body.
4. KISS (Keep it simple, stupid.)
5. Kiss.
6. Yep,...*that* Rule #6. (From Wayne Dyer in *The Power of Intention*: "Don't take yourself so goddam seriously.")
7. No whining.
8. Keep it big, diverse, loose, and meaningful.
9. Let people be who they are (and love them anyway).
10. Learn all you can from THIS moment.

I hope you are as relieved as I am that things have lightened up.

Confessions of a Spiritual Pragmatist

I started out as a good Catholic girl. Too good. I wanted to be a saint when I grew up. I read saints' biographies. I prayed to them. I even practiced putting my hands on my chest in holy bliss like St. Therese, the Little Flower of Jesus, did in the picture on the holy card. Stop laughing. I was serious. I wanted so badly to be "good."

By seventh grade, I was about the most disgusting version of a teacher's pet you could find. Sister Borromeo thought the sun rose and set in me. I did *everything* she asked me to do, including ratting on my classmates. Pathetic, but true.

Then I had an epiphany. In an instant one evening at home, I realized being her darling was not what I wanted at all. No one liked me. I wasn't having any fun. And I wasn't learning anything particularly useful with the effort. I knew how to please one nun. Nobody liked her either. What was that going to get me?

I stopped. Just like that. The day before, I was tattling on the kids who talked in "my row." But after I saw it for what it was, I was different. Done with that version of my life. I sassed the nun who'd made me her lieutenant in front of the entire class. I mean *really* sassed her.

As soon as I changed, other things changed. I was stripped of my rank as an official class fink. I didn't get to sit at the end of the row anymore. It didn't bother me at all. I had just turned my life upside down and was immensely pleased with myself. Two days later, I got invited to a dance one of the girls was hosting. And when I went, boys actually asked to dance with me. Years later, I heard a rumor that this hostess sometimes offered guys 25 cents a dance to dance with a particular girl. But at this point in my life, even that looks like a major victory. If it happened for me at that dance, she cared enough about whether I had to a good time to bribe the guys. Cool.

But back to seventh grade…. That was my first experience with what I have come to call spiritual pragmatism. I believe what works. If my life is better when I believe a certain way, then I will continue to accept those tenets of faith that got me there. If my life is going in the wrong direction, it's time to see if what I am believing is on target.

I believe in God. My life is infinitely better when I do. There is no guarantee I am "right." That I have the Truth properly defined and accurately inserted into how I choose to live. There is no guarantee the name I am using for that life force is even "correct." At first, I referred to this being as "God." Then I decided that had too much baggage and made me prone to visions of white haired men when I tried to talk to "Him." So I started to refer to the life force as "the Universe." The "Divine" is pretty non-committal, so I tried that for a while, too. That's good in PC situations.

Then I decided to get "cute." The force of all good in my life became ATI—"All There Is." I quit that when a good friend who seemed pretty relaxed about most things suggested God might not like a nickname. (I still think God liked it as much as I did, but it wasn't so important that I took a stand on it.) After that, I had a spell where I made the deity feminine—Goddess. That is as reasonable as the male moniker, but the images got in my way again. Now I had Earth Mother kinds of visions instead of the flowing white male hair. Too much of a distraction. At this point, I'm back to "God"—as Julia Cameron defines Him/Her/It: Good Orderly Direction. Or sometimes God/dess. But I worry that I'm being too technical with that—it looks like a beta for some kind of software. God may have been okay with ATI, but I suspect God/dess makes S/He groan.

While I was working on the name thing, I was working on other aspects. After a lot of variations, I have concluded we are each a part of God. When I think that way, my life is better. It's easier to accept other people's behavior. It *feels* better because there's no bona fide aloneness. This one makes sense to me. Why would God leave anyone out?

Of course, my sense of God's personality is my choice, too. My God is friendly. I can crawl up in the Divine Lap whenever I need to—for a nap, a cuddle, or a good cry. My God cares, but doesn't meddle. We agreed what I was here to do before I showed up, and it's my job to do it. I get help when I *ask*. Otherwise, I'm just going to do it my way. Well, usually. Sometimes I do need a whack with the divine two by four to get me back on track.

There's a law in science called the Law of Parsimony. According to that law, the correct explanation for a phenomenon is the simplest one. That's another reason to believe we're all little pieces of God, in my book anyway. It makes such simple, perfect sense to all be in this together. But the bottom line for me is still that it works.

I also find great workability in the tenet "Everything happens the way it's supposed to." When I accept that, little disappoints me and little rattles me. Sure, I still have to figure out what my role is in what's happening, but I don't need to control it. It's doing just fine without me. I found that out by trying it. Occasionally I have to learn the lesson again when I "fall off the wagon" and reenlist as Queen of Quite a Lot. But for the most part, it serves me very well.

Looking for the lesson in things that happen to me helps me stay focused on this moment. So that's another keeper. Looking for what I can learn from what I have to deal with gives it a purpose as I seek to honor my own purpose. I seek the lessons in everything. I learn a lot that way.

A related tenet is "There's a reason for everything." I don't subscribe to that one anymore. Reason implies a rational base, and spirituality is not limited to the mind. Also, the unspeakable things that happen have no rational justification. They happen. They are awful, and we all wish whatever it was had *not* happened. But it did. Now what can we take away from what happened? How can we make it useful by learning from it? A reason isn't needed for a lesson to be available.

At one point, I thought God orchestrated all these lessons. Now I don't need to rely on that. We are the ones who need to believe someone has to be in control. I'm not so sure God is into control. God is into living *this* moment well. The lesson doesn't have to be a nice logical conclusion with lovely symmetry. It's just an insight you gain from what you are doing—something to learn from whatever happens. There's some way to grow in whatever becomes part of your life. Even the stuff that left me so hollow and trampled had lessons. I was there for so long because I wasn't learning them. I was just enduring the situation. Once I started learning the lessons, things changed—just like with Sister Borromeo in the seventh grade.

When I work from this belief, my life is better. It makes more sense. The moments are richer with meaning. I'm calmer. I'm more alive. So I'm keeping it.

Recently, I've started working with accepting the truth that even those who come to bring the Light, will sometimes cast a shadow. No matter how hard I try, there are going to be times when I block that light for someone—when I *cause* a shadow for someone else. Accepting that truth helps me shift from struggling to never have it happen—which is impossible—to being able to notice when I do it and remedy it as best I can. Accepting there will be times when I am wrong is incredibly soothing. And knowing it happens for all of us makes it easier to be gracious with others when they cast shadows over me.

Sometimes, the seeds of what I choose to believe come from a different dimension of my life. Screenwriting helped me see the importance of conflict. The *necessity* of conflict. A good story *must* have conflict. A great story has multiple sources of tension. This is true of life as well. There is very little challenge in living when everyone needs the same thing and agrees on everything. Conflict is what gets the juices flowing on how to create something more—to solve the problem in a way that meets multiple sets of needs. It makes us use our heads to hone our negotiating skills and our communication skills. And we get to practice empathy.

In the world of fiction writing, conflict is king. When I started writing novels, my mentor exhorted "Conflict on every page." He was right, but it was hard to do. We live in a society that expects everyone to get along. That's not only unrealistic, it's unwise. We need to test our skills and that's done with an adversary. We need to meet resistance to grow. A kite rises against the wind. A seed only sprouts if there's dirt over it.

I could probably find 10 more beliefs to list and talk about, but you get the drift. I believe whatever makes my life work better. And I have absolutely no compunction to prove to you that it's "correct" or "right" or "the Truth." It just works for me. That's all I need.

There is one other part to this that I need to mention. It has to do with tools. I have found that, particularly in things spiritual, the tools keep changing. My insights have come through thinking, through dance, through long walks. They have also come by way of what I call "magic books." These are the books that jump off the shelf at me somehow.

Most often these are books I find at the bookstore when I am there looking for something else. Occasionally, they come from friends. Last fall, I was in a difficult phase in my relationship with my older son. I couldn't understand why he didn't understand what I had just gone through. I called in a chit on a book I'd lent to a friend and she returned two books when she dropped by. The second one wasn't mine, but when I opened it, the answer I needed for the current problem was looking up at me from the page. I didn't even need to read the rest of the book.

Another thing about the search for meaning at the spiritual level is that the access can be outside your comfort zone. While we were doing The Drizzle Tolerance Test, I discovered energy medicine—but not because I was looking for it. When I realized I was getting into something very different than what I had expected, I could have backed away. But the opportunity had presented itself. ("Everything happens the way it's supposed to.") I scheduled a session with the energy practitioner. I learned more in that two hours than I had in six months of regular therapy.

I scheduled another session. We had not been at it 10 minutes when I sensed something very unnerving begin. She told me if we wanted to continue, we would have to go into a past life of mine. I didn't believe any of that stuff, but there it was, trying to get my attention. She asked if I wanted to go on with the session and I agreed. Again, the insight went far beyond what I could have gotten any other way. For me, the talk therapy had been like digging for gold underground with a hand chisel and pick. The stuff I did with my energy practitioner was like taking a high-speed elevator down to a 20-foot vein of solid gold.

My experience with transformative dance was similar. I went to the first session because I like to dance and I was tired of begging my then spouse to go out on the dance floor with me. This stuff did not require—or even allow—a partner. After one session, I was well aware it affected me much more deeply than simply getting a chance to groove to "Louie Louie."

The point I'm trying to make with all this is *try whatever comes into your life*. You don't need to plunk down thousands of dollars for long-term programs. But do check out what's there right now. Try a little. Try it when you meet it.

In fact, for me at least, making long term plans for stuff I need at the spiritual level usually backfires. I move from one thing to something totally different often. For a while, I found great calm in participating in a drum circle. For a while I did Morning Pages just as faithfully as Julia Cameron recommends. For a while I meditated an hour in the morning. At one point, I even did an indoor, at-home version of a vision quest to see what I could learn. (Not much. I learned I can sleep on the floor in my workroom for an entire night and not dream a damn thing.)

Try what appeals. Try the stuff that seems woo woo. Maybe it *is* woo woo. But woo woo isn't illegal. It's just unfamiliar. Spirit demands we go beyond the familiar. You can have fun as you do it. Life is for living—try everything that looks good on the buffet.

Chapter Eight

Cut List for the Whole Enchilada

W<small>E USED TO OWN A COUNTERTOP</small> manufacturing company. We made and installed countertops of all sizes and shapes. Some of the things the guys created were pretty impressive. It was never a matter of hauling a 10-foot countertop and an 8-foot countertop into a kitchen and screwing them wherever they would fit on the walls.

Most of the parts were cut before they left the shop. The only way to have things turn out right was to be accurate—really accurate—with those cuts. And, of course, the installer needed to have all the pieces there when he got to the work site. The skill of the installer was essential. But the accuracy and completeness of the instructions detailing what was part of the installation and how it needed to be cut were even more critical. This information was provided as what was called a "cut list."

Success when we got to installation started with the cut list that had been generated when the project was still a plan. A half-inch error on a measure could mean a remake. Failing to list one piece of the configuration meant the job had to be rescheduled for install after that piece was manufactured. Goofs were not fun for customers—which everyone felt bad about. And they certainly weren't profitable. That cut list *had* to be accurate and complete.

Think of your decisions about what you want to do next that same way. Being as accurate and complete as you can in deciding what you need will save you a lot of grief.

Right. This seems like a major policy shift. I've been telling you to just put down whatever came to mind—including the smart remarks and off-the-wall-comments—for seven chapters now. That was important and still is. Letting yourself be that loose gives you more room for the obscure but relevant information to work its way to the surface. Maybe that happened for you and maybe it didn't, but that was the purpose of the strategy—to give you the best chance of hearing yourself in the din of what we call "life."

Now it's time to take that jumble of information and see what it can do in terms of helping you see your future. We've been creating a pile of jigsaw puzzle pieces. This chapter is the attempt to fit them all together. For that we do need to be accurate and complete—as much so as we can anyway. So doing some soul searching in that regard is an added dimension for this chapter.

You still need to keep it light. Both in the sense of being inspired—maybe even brilliant—and in the sense of being easy to carry. Too dark and you want to go to sleep. Too heavy and you want to put it down. Notice what catches your attention in the first second or two in terms of how you might spend your time from now on. Those are the brightest prospects for the *authentic* you. Notice what's easy to pick up in your mind. Those are the things your heart wants you to take along.

Please also make a commitment to not getting too hung up on one specific version of a plan. These are the years of living flexibly. If an opportunity or interest pops up that you had no clue about when you did the plan, you don't want to rule it out simply because you've haven't already written it down. As I make my way through this wonderland, I'm in awe of the diverse opportunities that keep arriving unexpectedly in my life. I have the chance to ski in France next winter. I sure wouldn't have put that in any plan I came up with last spring. I'm in the middle of drafting my city's public art plan. Two years ago, the term "public art" wasn't even in my vocabulary.

And now, for a word about fun. This is an essential food group for your soul. Make sure you get your minimum daily requirement in what you plan to do next. Please don't confuse "fun" and "leisure" though. Fun often involves work. Fun makes you lose track of time. Fun sometimes causes you to forget where you are. Fun is seizing the moment and wringing all you can from it—whether you are washing windows with your sweetie (water fight, anyone?) or riding the carousel at the county fair.

Go for it. Live a little. Aw, hell, live a lot. That's what the whole thing is about.

A good friend from the gas industry sent me a Christmas card last year that said it so well I framed it and put it on my nightstand as a reminder. The card shows two good ol' boy cowboys sitting on sleds at the edge of the top of a canyon. The look on the one's face as much as says, "Ya ready?" Yep. I am.

I'm doing the dumb stuff these days—my personal equivalents of going over the edge of that canyon on a Flexible Flyer. Odd thing is, the only thing that's increased is my fun quotient. And the stories I have to tell. Nothing has broken so far—except that ridiculous sense of propriety I'd been living with for the last 20 years.

A Few More Words About Tools

Before we roll up our sleeves and get on with this, there are a few more tool concerns to go over. Networking is so important that we need to look at it in more detail than we did back in Chapter Two. And then there is a trio that would not have made much sense at that point: Keep going; do "the next thing"; and trust the outcome.

NETWORKING

We all have and need networks. A network is the web of personal friendships, business acquaintances, and family relationships that defines an individual's personal version of "community." Unless you are in sales and have been listening to the Rolodex Theory of Networking, most of what you have as a network is already real. But in case there are a few of you who've been collecting business cards and calling it your "network", let's go over some basics.

Networking isn't about who you know. It isn't even about who knows you. It's about who you help. Because that's what effective networks are based on. If you only use your network when you need something, it won't exist for long. Networks are built on good will and positive regard. Even if you're the most lovable moppet on the planet, people get tired of you after a while if you have your hand out every time they see you.

A few weeks ago, my son's stepson was describing how he'd handled three job offers he'd come up with for the summer between college graduation as an electrical engineer and starting graduate school. He's been a pretty quiet addition to our family, so his strategy surprised as well as delighted me. Instead of just turning down the two jobs he decided he didn't want, he told friends who were still looking for summer jobs about them. That's networking. He didn't need to take that extra step for himself. But by doing so, he made life better for the friends—who then had a chance at the open positions—and for the employers—who got to hear from two new qualified candidates because of their involvement with Eric.

Networking is connecting the person you know who needs something to the person you know who has that very thing. Networking is caring about the people you know. Once you move away from the people structures of work, networking is also likely to be a primary source of information about the industry you've been in and the best way to keep current. Networks lead you to new friends and resources to address new interests. Networking is the Super Glue of the retirement years. If we use it wisely, we can make a lot of stuff fit together really well for a long time.

So…existing network or new network? It depends on three things: Do you want to stay involved in the things you are now involved in? Do you want to live where you live now? Do you like these people?

If you like what you are doing and plan to stay involved in it after you leave the fulltime workforce, keeping your current network fresh is important. If you are going to live where you live now, then your current network will be part of your on-going success. But if you want to start over at something entirely different, want to live somewhere else, or just don't enjoy the folks you've been networking with of late, you have a network construction project on the horizon.

Lucky you. I'm serious. It's entirely too easy to insulate yourself after you leave the workforce. You have your routines. You watch your favorite shows. You don't have to talk to anybody—sometimes not even to your spouse. This is the direct route to depression or else a quasi existence as one of the living dead. As humans, we need people. Having to establish a new network makes you go out and find them.

So…how do you start? With whatever presents itself. This is where knowing yourself pays off handsomely. When you start to talk about the things that interest you—at a cocktail party, an after-service church event, or in line at the grocery store—you are going to attract people who also have those interests. Talking to those people will give you a better sense of the organizations that focus on those same interests in your area. You can also look for where they *might* be. Newspapers list groups that meet to pursue specific interests. And then, of course, there is the Internet—Font of All Needed Information or at least enough of it to get you started.

You never know where you are going to get a key piece of information. I found out about the ski club I now belong to from a woman I met with because she'd worked at a company I was interested in. The friend who linked us up—a consummate networker—thought we should know each other to talk about that line of work and that company. We have benefited from knowing each other—but for more than discussions of job opportunities.

That's the best fun of networking: You never know what it's going to lead to.

I'm working on the art plan project because my brother gave me a set of watercolors for Christmas. His gift made me finally sign up for classes—where I met one of the women involved in bringing public art to the city we both live in. I ended up with a career in the gas industry because I agreed to teach an off-site course in industrial psychology for the University of Nebraska at Omaha. I got into crewing for an amateur road racing team because I needed a presentation for something at work. The art director at work also managed and drove for the racing team.

Another reason networking is important once you retire is that it fosters a sense of connection we don't get on the job anymore. Knowing people you can call about topics that interest you implies a certain level of acceptance. And acceptance is a universal need. We all want to belong and are most motivated to belong to those groups that we are like.

Okay, so you are…shy….out of practice….have no idea how to start…. have no desire to do this. Fine. You can stay where you are. If you like where you are, then you're golden. If you don't—or if you need to do some things differently to get to what you want as your new lifestyle, then you are going to have to stick your neck out and get on with it. Start small. Talk with a new neighbor (or one who's lived next to you for 20 years whom you've not yet met). Talk to someone you don't know at church or the gym. Attend an informational meeting for a group that interests you. Call and ask questions of the person who's listed to provide information about something you'd like to do. It's Nike time. Just do it.

KEEP GOING

And then, keep going. That is important. For networking. For whatever you lay out as what you want to do. For life, all day every day. Keep going. Even when you are disappointed with the results. Even when you hate the thing you know you need to do next. Keep going. The tortoise was onto something in that race with the hare.

The effectiveness of maintaining a steady pace is brought home to me every time we hike in the mountains. You'd think going slower uphill and faster downhill would be reasonable, but it doesn't work as a hiking pace. Start out steady and stay that way and you will finish refreshed. Too fast or too slow and it will be all work. When it gets steep, take shorter steps, but keep your pace. The results are close to miraculous.

While we are talking about pace, let's talk about timing, too. There will be things you want to happen that simply do not happen. At least not yet. Nothing you do will make it so. Accept that. Sometimes, it's just not time for what you think it's time for. I am old enough to have kids whose kids could be having kids, yet I am not even a grandma yet. I can't change that. As I've wandered through the last 13 years, there were jobs I was sure I had to have and relationships I was sure were meant to be, none of which materialized. It was not time.

But while I was waiting for all stuff I *thought* should be there to materialize, other stuff was coming into my life. Friends who make a huge difference. Interests that keep me delighted. Experiences that have taken my breath away—in both awe and fear (but not simultaneously, thank God). Accept that everything you lay out is subject to change and may not actually be part of the grand plan you and God cooked up for you this time around. What you lay out *will* springboard you to whatever is though. So keep going—at a nice steady pace.

DO THE "NEXT THING"

The way you keep going is by doing the next thing. "The next thing" is my current favorite life management tool. Whenever I get overwhelmed with what I am trying to do, or what I want that isn't here yet, or what I need to do but have no clue how to do, I look for "the next thing." This book is a "next thing." When I finish drafting it, figuring out how to get it in print will be the next "next thing." Focusing on just that next step helps me in two ways. It gives me a way to keep going even if the overall project is so daunting it could paralyze me. And it gives me a small enough piece to work on that there's a reasonable probability I can get it done. And done well.

Sometimes the "next thing" appears out of nowhere. These are often the "try it on" opportunities for defining a good life. A couple months ago, I was surfing websites trying to figure out how people who need to make money without holding a regular fulltime job can do it. There was a website titled *www.funjobsreview.com* that made it sound easy. They claimed you could make $25 to $100 a survey just for answering a bunch of questions for people who needed to do market research. And...ta dah...if you enrolled before the following day via the link given on the website, you could get access to *all* these great opportunities for one low fee.

I spent about four hours—and $35—on this little adventure and had signed up with five companies by the end of the night. They advised you to sign up with at least a hundred. The next morning came with a nice dose of sanity. What was I thinking? I don't even hike the same trail twice in a season because I don't like to do the same thing over and over. Did I really want to sit at my computer and provide the same information again and again day after day? Of course not.

Just because you try it, doesn't mean you're going to like it.

A great resource for this "try it on" kind of experimentation is the book *Too Young to Retire* by Marika and Howard Stone and the related website *www.2young2retire.com*. They have all sorts of ideas on "retirement" careers to check out and opportunities to explore.

The key to "doing the next thing" well is staying open. If you're telling yourself how totally stupid what you are doing is the whole time you are checking it out, there's no way you're giving it a fair trial. If you are worried silly someone you know will discover what you are doing and laugh, save the experiment for after you've dealt with your need to fit other people's molds.

Be as open as possible. Don't judge the experience by expectations. Judge it by how you feel when you are doing it. Is it fun? Interesting? Exciting? Did you lose track of time? Did it make you laugh? Feel lighter? *Did you like it?* If so, what do you think made it a good fit? If not, what was it about the opportunity that turned you off?

This is easier when you have learned who you are. Then it's downright fun. But if you aren't sure of yourself yet, it's still something you want to do. Sometimes those "try it on" moments are miraculous. Stepping into something totally out of character, even when you are clueless about what you like, might move you toward authenticity at light speed.

TRUST THE OUTCOME

Life is a whole lot easier if you choose to believe it's all going to work out the way it's supposed to—and well. Wayne Dyer covers this thoroughly in *The Power of Intention*. It's up to you, of course. You get to believe whatever you want. But believing you have a purpose and that there are things you specifically are meant to do with your time after you leave the workforce makes for a much richer tapestry—even before you uncover them.

Trusting the outcome doesn't mean everything is always going to turn out the way you planned it. We'd miss so much of the good stuff in our lives if it went that way. We'd also miss some pain and some difficult lessons we'd have preferred not to have to learn. Reality is not always fun. But trusting that the outcome will be what you need keeps you focused on *finding* what you need. It's out there somewhere. Just keep going.

This time in our lives can be filled with a lot of "not me" moments, where you try things on that turn out not to be what you are about at all. I've had "not me" *years* where I tried on thing after thing after thing. It's extremely frustrating. But that's what I needed to be doing. I had to have that massive dose of it as part of the foundation from which I could write this book.

For you, there may be other reasons for enduring it. The thing I wish I would have known sooner is that there was nothing wrong with my character that precipitated the behavior. I felt wishy washy, ineffective, wimpy. I began to doubt my sense of commitment and my ability to follow through—both traits I've valued highly my entire adult life. Knowing that it's a *process* and that it comes with the territory would have helped a lot. So…don't question your character if you are changing your mind a lot as you work through all this. That version of indecisiveness is sort of the older years equivalent of acne. It will go away as you get farther into this stage of your life.

Think and Do

Well, here we are at that place I warned you about in the introduction. This is where we take a stab at putting everything you've been digging up into a framework to use in deciding what you want to do next. I am not going to pretend this will be a neat orderly document you can use forever. It's more like a snapshot than a genealogy report But it should be far more useful than the yawning abyss of "doing nothing" we are expected to use as a blueprint.

Also—and you knew I was going to say this—it's up to you. You get what you put into it. If you've been comfortable skimming the surface, you are going to have a shallow plan. If you've gone deeper into the hidden treasures of who you are, that information will help you shape something of more substance and satisfaction.

There is one more thing I need to make clear. *This is a dynamic process.* We are talking about your life here. The unexpected is to be expected. New opportunities will present themselves just when you finally have the old ones narrowed down. It still boils down to trusting your gut. The exercises in this chapter are a means of organizing all that gut level information so you can use it more easily. But it is not a replacement for listening to your inner wisdom.

Part of the essence of wisdom is knowing when to make things happen, when to let things happen, and when to not worry about what happens. This effort focuses on the first part—when you want and need to make things happen. Please keep in mind it is only part of a good life. Letting things happen opens us to what's beyond the realm of our current experience. Not worrying about what happens removes the need for control that gives us an overly tight grip on life and produces strangled results.

Okay…onward. The following framework is in reverse order to the sequence of chapters we just worked through. We start at the center this time—because what you value must reside at the core of any plan you create. There are two aspects to what we need to do here. The first is a map of who you are on the inside—your Map of Me. The second is a map of the territory you intend to inhabit—your Map of Ideal Reality.

Map of Me

Exercise 8.1—THIS I BELIEVE...

Write at least three sentences (or 20 pages if you prefer) about your personal philosophy.

What life is about: _____

_____

_____

_____

_____

Why I'm here personally: _____

_____

_____

_____

_____

What's important about what I do with my life:_____

_____

_____

_____

_____

_____

Exercise 8.2 — ME AT THE CORE

What I want to focus on…

Part I.

The kind of impact I want to have from here forward: _____

_____

_____

_____

Part II.

Three topics I get passionate about and why they get me going.
(These do not have to be "causes.")

Topic 1: _____

_____

_____

_____

Topic 2: _____

_____

_____

_____

Topic 3: _____

_____

_____

_____

Action I will/could take in these areas: _____

_____

_____

_____

Part III.

My Code of Honor: The Rules I currently live by: _____

_____

_____

_____

Part IV.

What I value about myself: _____

_____

_____

_____

How I want to express what I value in what I do from here on:_____

_____

_____

_____

My current competencies:
*Include skills, abilities, talents, and anything else about you that makes you feel capable of accomplishing something.*_____

_____

_____

_____

Competencies I want to learn or expand now:
*Include every area of interest that might be worth using your time to learn. It doesn't have to be something you think you might be able to make money at or do full time.*_____

_____

_____

_____

_____

How I will or might use what I already know or want to learn once I retire: _____

_____

_____

_____

Interests I enjoy now and want to pursue more extensively:_____

_____

_____

_____

Interests I enjoyed in the past that I want to get back into:_____

_____

_____

_____

New interests I want to try and maybe take up now:_____

_____

_____

_____

Current responsibilities I want or must continue to hold:_____

_____

_____

_____

Needs I have that I want to address now and how I'm going to do that:

_____

_____

_____

_____

Dreams and goals I want to pursue now:

_____

_____

_____

Part V.

Stuff I want/need to let go of or get rid of:

*List "things" you want to let go of, but also other kinds of "stuff" including organizations you want to pull away from, time commitments you need to let go of to move on smoothly, and other people's ideas of what you "should do." Think about this area in the way that works best for you, but think as broadly as you can.*_____

_____

_____

_____

_____

_____

Part VI.

In a Nutshell:

In 50 words or so, summarize who you are and what's important for you to do at this point in your life._____

_____

_____

_____

What areas do you need to work on to accomplish that and how do you want to do it?_____

_____

_____

_____

Map of Ideal Reality
Exercise 8.3—THE TIME THING

The date I will (or did) leave the workforce: _____.

The length of time I want after that to enjoy "doing nothing" before I get into something else: _____

_____

Projects and other things I want to do BEFORE I take on a new permanent lifestyle:

Include stuff like backpacking across Europe or joining the Peace Corps for a two-year stint as well as things like cleaning the garage. _____

_____

_____

The amount of routine I want—where I do or am expected to do the same things at the same time regularly—after I leave my current job:

Include what you want as routines at home, but also what you are willing accept as routines to be part of things. For example, a golf or bowling league is likely to require a commitment to be in town to participate during the league's duration. How you want to shape your time commitment also represents a significant dimension in any work you might be considering. _____

_____

_____

_____

_____

_____

_____

_____

What I want my weekly calendar to look like:

	Sunday	Monday	Tuesday	Wednesday	Thursday	Friday	Saturday
morning							
afternoon							
evening							

What I want my monthly calendar to look like:

	Week 1	Week 2	Week 3	Week 4
Work:				
Family:				
Friends:				
Travel:				
Other:				

What I want my annual calendar to look like: (For example, do you want to go south for the winter, north for the summer, do income taxes for others, or play Santa as a seasonal business.)

JAN _____

FEB _____

MAR _____

APRIL _____

MAY _____

JUNE _____

JULY _____

AUG _____

SEPT _____

OCT _____

NOV _____

DEC _____

The amount of flexibility I want with my time/the amount of time structure I need:

How much lead time do you need to be able to take advantage of opportunities you value when they arise? How willing are you to drop what you are doing to meet a more important need that comes up—like a paid project or a family situation? Conversely, how much time structure do you NEED? Some need none and some are better off if they know they will be doing certain things at certain times every day or week. These needs are not "good" or "bad." It just helps to know where your comfort level is in terms of time. _____

_____

_____

_____

Exercise 8.4 — KNOWN OPPORTUNITIES

Things already on the horizon that I plan to get into more:
Include areas of interest you are already pursuing, commitments you want to make to your family and friends, transitions with your current work that will be part of your new lifestyle, volunteer efforts you have already been involved in, etc. These are things you have already begun to prepare for and for which you have some sense of the commitment you want to make. _____

_____

_____

_____

_____

What I need to put in place to be able to do that:
These could be things like taking a class, applying for a work visa, or getting business cards made. Are your finances set up so you can do this—things like automatic bill pay, self-deposit on income, etc.? Does doing this require you do some other part of your life differently? _____

_____

_____

_____

How I will expand/maintain my current network for doing these things:

_____

_____

_____

Areas of interest I want to BEGIN to explore:
Include ANYTHING that interests you—playing the cello, going back for a PhD in meteorology, starting an adult education program about bees, kayaking on the Zambezi, etc. _____

_____

_____

_____

How I'm going to start investigating these areas:

These actions can be huge or tiny. Some folks jump in on the deep end, and some like to just get their toes wet the first time or two. Be yourself in what you list to get started. _____

_____

_____

How I will build a network in these areas: _____

_____

_____

_____

Subtotal: WHAT I WANT MOST TO PURSUE AS PART OF WHAT I DO NEXT:

What do you want to be SURE is included in how you live your life from now on?

_____

_____

_____

Exercise 8.5—SUPPORT NEEDS AND RESOURCES

Ways my sense of competence is going to be reinforced:
How are you going to know you're good at whatever you are doing? Will there be someone there who's likely to tell you on a regular basis? Will you have tests to take or timelines to meet? Is there a score involved in what you want to do—as in golf, bowling, or bridge? _____

_____

_____

_____

_____

Friends/family and the advice or help each is best at:

Who will you turn to if you need help with something? Consider your whole range of needs—from someone to grouse to if it rains the day you wanted to hike to someone you can ask to help you get a new computer fully functioning. If you think there so no one to turn to, think again. Sometimes we inherit resources as part of our family. Sometimes we claim them by making friends. Sometimes we pay for them. Sometimes they appear miraculously just when we need them. Help comes in a broad range of varieties, but we ALL have some version of it if we choose to seek it and use it. _____

_____

_____

_____

_____

Organizations I plan to belong to that will help me feel connected and accepted:

Include only those groups you intend to PARTICIPATE in. No fair to count the Elks if you never go to meetings or your political party because you send them a check.

_____

_____

_____

How I am going to know I'm on track:

No one else is going to be paying much attention to your performance on this stuff. How are you going to keep yourself on track and feeling good about your accomplishments? It can be as structured as a monthly progress report to yourself or as loose as a daily "gut check" before you turn out the light. But set up something to help yourself know you are doing what you need to do to make it the life you want. _____

_____

_____

_____

Bottom Line of the Whole Enchilada:

Now boil it down to where you can explain it to someone in two minutes at a cocktail party. This is not why we did all this, but the exercise is great for increasing the clarity of your thinking.

This is what I'm going to do: _____

_____

_____

This is how I am going to do it: _____

_____

_____

To those of you who wrote on those last 10 lines with confidence, YEAH! To those of you who didn't, fear not. You're not alone, and it's not the end of the world. This exercise tells you a lot, no matter how far along you are. If you don't have it all figured out, you still know more—a LOT more—than when you started. "Not getting it" will only happen if you give up on figuring it out.

For those of you who want to look for a "different teacher" at this point, *Don't Stop the Career Clock* by Helen Harkness, *Too Young to Retire* by Marika and Howard Stone, *Live the Life You Love* by Barbara Sher, or *Don't Retire, Rewire* by Jeri Sedlar and Rick Miners might be useful.

But if you don't want more books and are still in the fog, start with a gut check. What are you feeling? Are you tight? Slack? Ready to jump off the bridge because of the anxiety of not being able to figure it out? Work you way from understanding that to figuring out what's prompting the sensation. There is probably something you don't want to deal with that's keeping you from getting into the rest of your life joyfully. Sometimes it's as straightforward as admitting you don't really want to retire at all. Sometimes it's a complicated personal situation that might require professional help to get through.

The essential thing here is to know yourself. Any way you can find to do that is a good way. (However drugs and alcohol are masks, not ways to access your authenticity, so don't bother to go there.)

Naked Truths and Roundabouts

And now, for a confession. For the first time in this book, I am resorting to Plan B on this part of a chapter. In all the other chapters, what ended up on the page the first time turned out to be the right content. The words often needed considerable help, but the topics were on target. This time, the topics of the anecdotal part didn't work.

Plan A was to offer you *mibble.2*—my completion of the exercises so you had an example to use. I did them. Really. I did. But when I read them over, they weren't that interesting. They taught me some good things, but they didn't have a whole lot of meat for anyone else.

At first, I thought it was because I've already given you a megadose of information about me. About the only thing I haven't told you is my shoe size. Maybe you just didn't need to know any more about me.

But as I got thinking about my own experience doing this chapter's exercises, I realized it wasn't about the "mbl" in it at all. The value of the work is largely in the process not the product with this. Much as having a clearer idea of what you want to do with these magical years is invigorating, *looking* at it is what's the most important. The plans will change. The process is what will help you do that readily, easily, and comfortably. You've mastered a new way of addressing this challenge. Working through this book, you've acquired new tools for exploring the delightful and uncharted territory of yourself. Who you are now. What you like. Need. Hope to do. Where you want to go. How you want to live. Taking the time to ask yourself these questions is the key to the realm.

Having the courage to endure the thundering silence that results the first few times you attempt the process is also important. The first attempts are likely to involve a lot of that. The answers come if you keep asking the questions and listening to the silence at the center of yourself.

The bottom line is to deal well with what is right in front of you. Do that thing well and the next thing will present itself. Do the next thing well and some other opportunity will unfold. It's not like the progression of job titles that's almost automatic for those within some disciplines. It's not a function of time in grade. It's a function of how persistent you are in working on it. And how patient you are with not figuring it all out in an afternoon.

You attract what you think about. You *become* what you think about according to Earl Nightingale. So think about what you like and enjoy. Think about a lifestyle that pleases you no end. Think big. Think happy. Keep thinking about it day after day even when you feel like you are swimming in driller's mud.

The framework you just worked through was worth doing. There were some surprises, right? I was amazed to find myself setting a drop-dead date for when I would resort to self-publishing this book. I hadn't realized I was considering it. I learned I value physical activity even more than I realized and that I need routine mostly first thing in the morning. Useful to know. Not earth shattering, but helpful for being as good to myself as I can be. It's good to know a lot about yourself.

And I do. But there is always something more to learn. After you've been working at this mapping process for a while, it doesn't require such a formal structure though. If you've been paying attention to yourself all along, it boils down to three questions when you have the chance for a major redirect as you do when retirement is an option:

- What do I want more of in my life?

- What do I want less of in my life?

- How do I make that happen?

As you proceed, take a lesson from my city's traffic engineers. Roundabouts are a hot topic here. We have a lot of them because the city believes in "traffic calming." It also believes in making cost effective choices. Traffic circles cost less to maintain (no expenses for traffic lights), are prettier, keep traffic moving (at least if people drive them properly) and use less gas. (No one sits alone at the intersection with the engine idling waiting for the light to change.) Everyone should love them, right?

Residents regularly call City Hall to complain. Much of the population is convinced roundabouts are "dangerous" for all kinds of reasons. If you fill the center of the roundabout with art and vegetation, it becomes even more "dangerous." Any fool knows you have to see the oncoming traffic across the intersection.

Many of you seasoned drivers are nodding your heads in agreement, right? Of course a clear view of oncoming traffic is essential.

No. Not really. Not in a roundabout. The traffic you need to worry about is to your left (at least if you are driving on the right like we do in the United States). The vehicles across the roundabout aren't a factor for you and won't be to where you are on the circle until well after you are into the flow of traffic—IF there is no one to your left. That's what you need to be looking at. But after years of "practice" many locals still come to a total stop when the roundabout is clear because someone is *approaching* it from the opposite direction. So much for that extra efficiency.

Roundabouts are a new situation for those of us who grew up in the land of stoplights. This next stage of life is a new situation for us, too. There will be a lot of well-meaning people who are going to encourage you wait for that approaching traffic because they don't really understand how things work best at this stage of life. They will envy your leisure time and covet your chance to sit in that rocking chair. They will be excited for you because you can *claim* the rocking chair. They are your friends, families, and coworkers. They are so happy for you—and so envious of your opportunity to do nothing. Before you know it, you'll be sitting in the damn chair.

The more you know about yourself, the less you will believe them. The more you know about what you want, the easier it is to merge into the flow of life and go where you want to go next.

Chapter Nine

Choose Your Own Adventure

WHEN MY BOYS WERE STUDENT READERS, they enjoyed a series of books called *Choose Your Own Adventure*. The books were set up so the reader got to decide what the hero was going to do about the situation in the story. You resumed reading on the page that told the story with your version of the decision as part of it. This happened periodically throughout the book, so the story you ended up reading was uniquely yours.

What a great analogy for Life. Even if we start with the same book, we all get to choose our own adventure.

As we come to the end of our time together, it would be good to dwell on that a bit. What do *you* want as an adventure? Some of us are content with a walk around the block occasionally. Some of us literally need to take a trip into outer space. Regardless, the critical element is *choice*. Things are going to happen in your life whether you step up to the decisions or not. But if you choose—and choose according to who you really are now, it's going to fit you a whole lot better. You don't wear someone else's shoes very often. Why would you pick up an old, worn out version of "life after 60" and wear that?

This choosing is not always easy. So much of our lives has been focused on others. So much of what we are now might still need to be discovered. Not knowing can feel so….well…..stupid.

Not knowing. This is another paradoxical gift of this time of our lives. Not knowing is what makes us most human. Not knowing and being willing to search for the answers we don't have yet takes us to new understanding of all manner of things. It is the quintessence of being human. Still, it gets a really bad rap.

There is nothing wrong with not knowing.

There is everything wrong with not *wanting* to know. Mark the difference.

In a short chapter in *Office Hours,* Walter Kiechel III suggests "Imagine a test…of how far you are likely to get in your career…your accomplishments…what you and your spouse really feel for each other…whether you have unexploited talents…how large your position figures in what others and you think of yourself. You will probably take such a test. It's called retirement." He goes on to note most people flunk and that the rest of society barely notices. Even more distressing is he said this in 1988. We haven't done much to remedy this situation in the last two decades.

It's time to wake up. Smell the roses. But also the coffee.

We need to figure this stuff out, individually and collectively. Squandering 40 percent of anything else would be unthinkable. Why are we willing to squander as much as forty percent of our LIVES? Leaving the workforce is not the same as leaving the planet. Figure it out. Use whatever methods present themselves. But be patient, too. Sometimes, it's just not time for what you're waiting for to sprout.

A few years ago a young Navy officer and his wife moved into the house three doors down from ours. The neighborhood prided itself on being friendly and we gave our all to help them learn the best ways to accomplish what was needed in their new environment. The husband was particularly grateful for this help since he was shipping out for a stint in the Middle East almost immediately.

When he returned from his tour, he came around the neighborhood with little gifts to show his appreciation—bits of root stock for plants from Hawaii. He bought them while the ship was in port in Honolulu. He gave me two because people had told him how much I liked to garden.

I read up on how to plant the roots, bought special soil, and put them in pots. One was a variety of orchid, and the other was a ginger plant. I was particularly excited about the ginger plant because I'd never seen one grown as a houseplant.

I put them in the "best" window and tried to follow the instructions precisely. After about a month and a half, the orchid sent up a little shoot. I was delighted. Having something you planted in dirt emerge as a green living thing is a quiet but solid link to the Divine. The little orchid shoot held it's own and started to grow. I kept checking the ginger plant. Nothing. Then still nothing.

After about six months of having it sit lifeless in my kitchen window, I accepted defeat. I had failed with the ginger. I put the pot out in the garage, intending to empty it to use for something else. Life got busy and I never got back to the pot.

Four months later, we decided to clean the garage. I grabbed the pot, intending to put the dirt in one of the flowerbeds. And there, waiting to be discovered, was a lovely green shoot! A ginger plant. Amazing. No water. No light. For four months. But there it was, ready to give life a go.

So I took it in the house, gave it some water, and put it in the window. It flourished.

I brought it with me when I moved to this house. It's big now. I will have to transplant it soon. It has beautiful green leaves and—if I am patient—will bloom eventually.

But nothing happened for so long that I gave up on it. It came back into my life on its own when it was ready, not when I was focused on making it happen.

There is great wisdom in accepting you can't make everything happen when you want it to. You can't make some things happen at all. But you can trust that what you *really* need to happen—regardless of what you are telling yourself needs to happen—will.

For me, that means it's time to de-emphasize action planning and annual goals. This sounds counterintuitive, given I have been lobbying for more focus on what we want to do with this part of our lives. But it's not. We don't need to plan so much as to DO. My plan is to do the next thing. I have to know myself well enough to look for a "next thing" that reflects who I really am. But I don't have to lay out all the steps to where I want to be in 10 years. I need to know where to start and then let the flow of life have control of what comes in when.

Relinquishing control. "Whoa!" I can hear you saying it even though I'm not anywhere near you.

Let's get real, folks. We never had it in the first place. We do all that action planning stuff to THINK we have it. Don't get me wrong. For a rationally based project, for a work effort that requires a lot of people knowing what is supposed to happen when, for big galas like formal weddings, plans are critical. But for figuring out what you are going to do with the rest of your life, they're way too limiting.

This is a particularly important insight for those who are retiring from executive positions. The need to control everything will not be in your best interest in the new environment. Executive management entails a lot of control. Pay attention to when and how you apply it once you are away from that context.

There are a few other things it would be wise to realize will be special challenges for retiring executives. You're used to having other people honor your direction for how to get things done. When you leave the corner office, all that changes. Be ready to learn to value yourself in new ways. Also, you most likely will have enough money you don't "need" to work. This is not a plus. It just increases the number of options available and the potential for scuttling a new "job" if you don't like it right away. You are also likely to be one of those people who values facts and expects a pie chart to back up every observation. Learning to rely on your intuition might be hard at first.

Regardless of what you've done as a vocation, the basic challenge is the same. GET TO KNOW YOURSELF. No matter who you are. Whether you have enough money to retire or you are going to have to work until you are 98. Know yourself. If you know what you like, you can find a job that includes it. Then it's fun. It makes your life bigger. If you know what you like, you can use it to keep yourself healthy. If you know who you are and what you believe in, the "yes's" and the "no's" fall in the right places more easily. Know yourself.

I was going to write about balance, but I'm not sure it applies. Most of us have spent our lives up until now keeping a lot of balls in the air. We've been trying to maintain equilibrium—between work and home, personal needs and commitments to others, getting things done and being able to relax—ever since we became "adults." Things change at this point. Balance is still important, but there is room now to let passion cause things get a bit lopsided occasionally.

You are not going to get in trouble at work if you stay up all night finishing the dollhouse you started to build or the chapter you wanted to outline. No one is going to take you aside and tell you to focus on "the important things" if your time is your own and you want to spend it birding. We can be more in love with whatever we are doing when we graduate to retirement. We can be intense to the point of not sleeping much while we are working on it. We can put it aside for three years. It's totally up to us to define how we want to approach whatever we decide on.

So in lieu of balance, let's try for honesty. Then the focus will always be on what's important. There will be people who think that since you "don't work" your time is theirs. If you don't agree, tell them so. There will be people who invite you to do what they love. If you aren't really interested, admit it. Find the friends who let you be who you really are. Respect them that same way.

Don't be afraid to try things on. When you have finally found the right clothes, you know it. I learned this on one particular bargain hunting expedition with my retail savvy older sister. I personally am one of the top five worst shoppers in the nation. When I saw a cute sleeveless black and white dress on the rack and took it to the dressing room, it was new behavior for me. Deciding to try something on was a major skill improvement.

When I put it over my head and first caught a glimpse of myself in it, I knew instantly it was mine. No logic required. I looked like me in it. A really nice version of me. The same thing happens with life. Feeling like YOU in what you are experiencing is when all the looking pays off. You are alive. The fit is perfect. You could not imagine yourself in anything else that would work as well.

If you keep trying things on, the clarity will come. Yes! This is ME. I need to do this…learn this…create this…give this to the world. Once you find it, your life focuses better than the Hubble telescope. Keep going in the meantime.

There are a few other things I'd like to touch on. Life is messy. There is no way around that. And that's okay. Getting dirt on your hands is a good thing. Remember when getting muddy was the best part of the fun? Let's hear it for messes. Creative chaos is essential. Nothing worth doing gets done without making a mess at some point.

Do think about what you want to do and what's needed to do it. But forget the big elaborate plans. If you want to come up with a plan that impresses your friends or your spouse, go make a mess instead. You aren't ready. Real, workable plans are usually fairly sparse. They leave big spaces to accommodate all those unanticipated delights and opportunities that are part of really living. Big elaborate plans are a waste of time. If they aren't authentic, they're useless and are usually too heavy to carry with you. They end up on the shelf with the other curios.

Learn to love yo yo's. They are mandatory equipment at this point for most of us. Remember when whatever your kid was doing—that drove you nuts—was considered a "phase?" Well…. indecision is part of this phase. It's like "the terrible twos" only it lasts until you figure out your purpose instead of until your next birthday.

Ignore the siren's song of youth and focus instead on vibrance. It doesn't fade, has a much longer shelf life, and boasts a whole lot more uses. It's also smarter, wiser, and has more fun.

Have the courage to do what you came to do. Don't believe the ads— on TV, in magazines, on your computer. You know more about what you need than they could ever fathom. And, believe me, they don't really want to know what you need. They're going to spend their last advertising dollar trying to convince you that you need what they want to sell.

When you find your purpose, you will have a certainty that stupefies you. It's not just a case of "maybe." You will know with every fiber of your being it's the right thing for you to do.

To get there, keep learning about yourself. Keep doing the next thing. Get ready to launch. Not even the sky is the limit.

Chapter Notes

Chapter One

1. Lim, Paul, J. "7 Reasons NOT to Retire," *US News & World Report*. Money & Business Annual Retirement Guide. June 12, 2006. Includes information from the Merrill Lynch studies.

2. Schlesinger, Robert. "An Expert's View of Ageism: Things Aren't Any Better," *AARP Bulletin*, June, 2006, reports on research on ageism done by Robert Butler, and the International Longevity Center.

3. Kanter, Rosabeth Moss. "Back to College," *AARP, The Magazine*, July&August, 2006.

4. *Merriam Webster's Collegiate Dictionary*, Tenth Edition, Merriam-Webster, Inc., 1993.

5. *AARP Bulletin*, June, 2006, quoted Hugh Hefner (as did the local newspaper and AOL news online).

6. Harkness, Helen. *Don't Stop the Career Clock: Rejecting the Myths of Aging for a New Way to Work in the 21st Century*, Davies-Black Publishing, 1999.

7. Geissl, Theodore (Dr. Seuess). *Oh, the Places You'll Go!*, Random House, 1990.

8. "7 Reasons NOT to Retire" (See citation #1.)

9. Unexpected retirement statistic quoted in "numbers box" on page 32, *AARP, The Magazine*, September&October, 2006.

10. *The Runaway Bride*, movie starring Richard Gere and Julia Roberts, 1999.

Chapter Two

1. Sher, Barbara. *Live the Life You Love: In Ten Step-by-Step Lessons,* Dell Publishing, 1996.

2. Kepner, Charles, H. and Tregoe, Benjamin B. *The Rational Manager: A Systematic Approach to Problem Solving and Decision Making,* Kepner-Tregoe, Inc., 1965.

3. Gladwell, Malcolm. *Blink: The Power of Thinking Without Thinking,* Little Brown and Company, 2005.

4. Dyer, Wayne. A comment made in both live performances for PBS and on the Insight series done for Nightingale-Conant.

5. Gawain, Shakti. *Developing Intuition: Practical Guidance for Daily Life,* New World Library, 2000.

6. Dossey, Larry. *Reinventing Medicine: Beyond Mind-Body to a New Era of Healing,* Harper San Francisco, 1999.

7. Myss, Caroline. *Anatomy of the Spirit: The Seven Stages of Power and Healing,* Three Rivers Press, 1996.

Chapter Three

1. Heimer, Matthew, and Bellstrom, Kristen. "Retire Happy," *Smart Money,* April, 2006.

2. The Society for Human Resource Management study is discussed in the Heimer and Bellstrom article. (See Note 1 of Chapter Three.)

3. Lim, Paul, J. "7 Reasons NOT to Retire," *US News & World Report.* Money & Business Annual Retirement Guide. June 12, 2006, cites the Ernst and Young/Human Capital Institute study.

4. Lloyd, Carol. *Creating a Life Worth Living,* Harper Perennial, 1997

5. Cyrus, Billy Ray. As quoted in *USA Magazine,* June 18, 2006, page 2.

6. Kirshenbaum, Mira. *Too Good to Leave Too Bad to Stay,* Penguin Books, 1997.

7. Patricia Evans. *The Verbally Abusive Relationship*, Adams Media Corporation, 1992, 1996.

8. Lerner, Harriet. *The Dance of Connection: How to Talk to Someone When You're Mad, Hurt, Scared, Frustrated, Insulted, Betrayed, or Desperate*, Quill/Harper Collins, 2002.

9. Myss, Caroline. *Anatomy of the Spirit: The Seven Stages of Power and Healing*, Three Rivers Press, 1996.

10. Clements, Jonathan. "Getting Going," *The Wall Street Journal Sunday*, June 18, 2006.

11. Kelly, Matthew. *The Rhythm of Life: Living Every Day with Passion and Purpose*, Fireside, 1999.

12. Ellerbee, Linda. "Being Sixty: A New Age for Aquarians," *AARP, The Magazine*, July& August, 2006.

13. Harkness, Helen. *Don't Stop the Career Clock: Rejecting the Myths of Aging for a New Way to Work in the 21st Century*, Davies-Black Publishing, 1999.

14. Selye, Hans. *The Stress of Life*, 1978.

15. Myss, Caroline. *Why People Don't Heal and How They Can*, Harmony Books, 1997.

Chapter Four

1. Roth, Geneen. "About the 'E' Word", *Prevention*, July 2006. pages 86-87.

2. Loehr, Jim and Schwartz, Tony. *The Power of Full Engagement: Managing Energy, Not Time, Is the Key to High Performance and Personal Renewal*, Free Press, 2003.

3. Dychtwald, Ken. *Age Power: How the 21st Century Will Be Ruled by the New Old*, Jeremy Tarcher/Putnam, 1999. Page 91.

4. The Institute of Noetic Sciences was founded by astronaut Edgar Mitchell and maintains a website at www.noetic.org.

5.   Examples of titles by these authors on topics in this realm include:

Chopra, Deepak. *The Book of Secrets: Unlocking the Hidden Dimensions of Your Life*, Random House, 2004.

Dossey, Larry. *The Extraordinary Healing Power of Ordinary Things: Fourteen Natural Steps to Health and Happiness*, HarperCollins, 2006.

Siegel, Bernie. *Peace, Love, and Healing: Bodymind Communication & the Path to Self Healing: An Exploration*, HarperCollins, 1990.

6.   Kratz, Ellen Florian. "Where to Retire in Style," *Fortune*, June 26, 2006.

7.   Home Depot "south for the winter" program was mentioned in Lim, Paul, J. "7 Reasons NOT to Retire," *US News & World Report*. Money & Business Annual Retirement Guide. June 12, 2006.

8.   Earthwatch Institute can be contacted at (800)776-0188 or *www. earthwatch.org*. They offer a catalog of opportunities where participants pay to be part of scientific projects in remote places.

9.   Harkness, Helen. *Don't Stop the Career Clock: Rejecting the Myths of Aging for a New Way to Work in the 21st Century*, Davies-Black Publishing, 1999.

Chapter Five

1.   Ludlum, Robert. *The Bourne Identity*, 1984.

2.   Comfort, A. "Senility—Is It Mostly a Self-Fulfilling Prophecy?" *Mind/Brain Bulletin 6*, Jan 26, 1981, as reported in Harkness.

3.   Harkness, Helen. *Don't Stop the Career Clock: Rejecting the Myths of Aging for a New Way to Work in the 21st Century*, Davies-Black Publishing, 1999.

4.   Carlin, George. This quote has been floating around for a while, it may have originally appeared in *Brain Droppings*, Hyperion, 1997.

5.   Kanter, Rosabeth Moss. "Back to College," *AARP, The Magazine*, July&August, 2006.

6. Mandela, Nelson. I've found this quote both standing alone and attributed to him in other sources. The primary source is indefinite.

7. Armstrong, Thomas. *7 Kinds of Smart: Identifying and Developing Your Many Intelligences*, Plume/Penguin, 1993.

8. Doerr, Harriet. *Stones for Ibarra*, Penguin, 1978.

9. Auel, Jean. *The Clan of the Cave Bear*, Crown, 1980.

10. Cafazzo, Debbie. "Can You Pass Citizenship Test?" *The Tacoma News Tribune*, July 4, 2006

Chapter Six

1. Perls, Frits. was a psychotherapist who created both books and audiotapes dealing with emotional authenticity.

2. McKay, Matthew, Rogers, Peter, and McKay, Judith. *When Anger Hurts*, New Harbinger Publications, 1989.

3. Roosevelt, Eleanor. As quoted on a magnet on my brother Steve's refrigerator.

4. These psychology experiments are oft mentioned in introductory psych lectures and other such initial forays into the realm of science and psyche. I could not confirm who actually did them or where, but they were already being described in basic psychology texts in 1977.

5. Mahoney, Sarah. "The Secret Lives of Single Women," *AARP, The Magazine*, May&June 2006.

6. Wanzenried, Lucy Franks. As noted in conversation regarding her doctoral dissertation work in gerontology at the University of Nebraska.

7. Northrup, Christiane, M.D. *The Wisdom of Menopause*, Bantam Books, 2001.

8. Kanter, Rosabeth Moss. "Back to College," *AARP, The Magazine*, July&August, 2006.

9. Ruby, Margaret. Material presented in advanced courses of *DNA: Integration & Reprogramming*, Possibilities Vocational School, February, 2002.

10. Roosevelt, Eleanor. This one came in a Page-A-Day calendar a few years ago.

11. Dyer, Wayne W. *Your Erroneous Zones*, 1971.

Chapter Seven

1. Harkness, Helen. *Don't Stop the Career Clock: Rejecting the Myths of Aging for a New Way to Work in the 21st Century,* Davies-Black Publishing, 1999.

2. Cameron, Julia. *The Artist's Way: A Spiritual Path to Higher Creativity*, J.P. Putnam's Sons, 1992.

3. Dreaver, Jim. *The Ultimate Cure: The Healing Energy Within You*, Llewellyn Publications, 1996.

4. Braden, Gregg. *Walking Between the Worlds: The Science of Compassion*, Radio Bookstore Press, 1997.

5. "Majority Believe in God—Just Not the Same One." Article from the *Los Angeles Times* as printed in the *Tacoma News Tribune*, Sept. 17, 2006.

6. Schwartz, Tony. *What Really Matters: Searching for Wisdom in America*, Bantam Books, 1995.

7. Sher, Barbara. *I Could Do Anything, if I Only Knew What It Was*, Delacorte Press, 1994.

8. Myss, Caroline. *Sacred Contracts: Awakening Your Divine Potential*, Harmony Books, 2001.

9. *The Essential Rumi*, translated by Coleman Barks, HarperCollins, 1995.

10. Myss, Caroline. *Anatomy of the Spirit: The Seven Stages of Power and Healing*, Three Rivers Press, 1996.

11. Dyer, Wayne. *The Power of Intention: Learning to Co-create Your World Your Way*, Hay House, 2004.

Chapter Eight

1. Stone, Marika and Howard. *Too Young to Retire: 101 Ways to Start the Rest of Your Life*, Plume/Penguin, 2002.

2. Dyer, Wayne. *The Power of Intention: Learning to Co-create Your World Your Way*, Hay House, 2004.

3. Harkness, Helen. *Don't Stop the Career Clock: Rejecting the Myths of Aging for a New Way to Work in the 21st Century*, Davies-Black Publishing, 1999.

4. Stone, Marika and Howard. *Too Young to Retire: 101 Ways to Start the Rest of Your Life*, Plume/Penguin, 2002.

5. Sher, Barbara. *Live the Life You Love: In Ten Step-by-Step Lessons*. Dell Publishing, 1996.

6. Sedlar, Jeri and Miners, Rick. *Don't Retire, REWIRE! 5 Steps to Fulfilling Work That Fuels Your Passion, Suits Your Personality or Fills Your Pocket*, Alpha/Penguin, 2003.

7. Nightingale, Earl. *The Strangest Secret*, an audiotape series offered by Nightingale-Conant, circa 1985.

Chapter Nine

1. The *Choose Your Own Adventure* series was developed and published by Chooseco, Warren, VT.

2. Walter Kiechel III. *Office Hours: A Guide to the Managerial Life*, Little, Brown and Company, 1988.

From Here, There, and Everywhere— Other Resources

This section is intended as a starter kit for your personal storehouse of information. Create your customized treasure trove. It will serve you well in crafting your own best life. Hopefully, as you add to it, it will have all manner of delightful things you might need eventually. Even more hopefully, these pages and your own additions will be organized just well enough that you can only find what you need with a bit of work.

I say that in all seriousness. It's good to have to look for what you need sometimes. Otherwise, you never find that indispensable stuff you don't know you need even more until you come across it. Some of the most useful books on my shelf are there because they were next to something I was actually looking for. Likewise, the best websites are often links, not where I went initially.

Books can be downright magical as resources. Some of my favorites seem to contain different—and perfectly targeted—information each time I go back to them. Even when the information I need this time is way different than what made them valuable in the first place. Some of them have literally jumped off the shelf at me in bookstores or libraries. Some have languished for years on my "to read" stack only to be embraced at a crucial moment when the information made a dramatic difference in my choices. Books seem to be one of the most versatile tools of the Divine in terms of offering timely nudges in my life. So I am particularly partial to books. Thus, the starter kit I provide here is long on book titles.

But books are only good resources for information that is not time-sensitive. Books take a long time to get into print when the traditional channels are followed. Much can change on a given subject while a contract is negotiated and the book is positioned in the printing and release schedules. The process often takes two years or more. So it's not wise to rely exclusively on books. But they are definitely my bedrock and the framework of whatever research I start to build.

What's more immediate? Periodicals come out monthly, sometimes weekly, sometimes daily. That information is more current hard copy than what you can find a book. So periodicals are of more value if you're looking for information that reflects THIS point in time—or the newest and greatest of anything.

And a good website trumps a periodical. I can know the ski conditions at my favorite resort as of this minute if I check their web cam. Websites are a newer tool and I'm not great at wringing the best out of them yet—but they are certainly the resource of the future. They can be real time in their reporting which is a huge benefit in many instances. There are several listed here that I find useful. Your own list will be a lot longer, both because you will discover those that help with what you want to keep track of, but also because this information source is growing exponentially.

But BEWARE. There are way too many websites that suggest they are current when they are not. At least periodicals include a publication date and issue number as a matter of course. Websites say "now" in what they present but that "now" could have been created five years ago and never updated. Likewise, check publication dates in the books you read. "The latest research on heart health" looks a lot different now than it did 10 years ago.

And while I am offering warnings, I will offer the first of several about using the Internet. There is much room for mischief there, so pay attention. Not everything is accurate or even true. Validate your sources before you make decisions with their information

And, while we are at it, let's admit this list itself will get old fast. We live in the Information Age. We have more coming at us daily than some centuries generated in total. To deal with that, additional entries and suggestions are included at *www.mining-silver.com*. (Please DO use that website! Information there has gone through my own screens and is updated frequently.)

Okay with all those caveats, here is the best of what I've met for living well.

BOOKS

Armstrong, Thomas. *7 Kinds of Smart: Identifying and Developing Your Many Intelligences*. Plume/Penguin, 1993.

> Helps debunk the idea "intelligence" is that intimidating verbal/ mathematical assessment the IQ score measures. True intelligence is not about qualifying for Mensa. Armstrong does a good job of giving us the broader picture.

Borysenko, Joan. *Fire in the Soul: A New Psychology of Spiritual Optimism*. Warner Books, 1993.

> Considers the crises in everyday lives that can either be seen as sources of fear or opportunities for growth, understanding, and deeper meaning. A pleasant read with anecdotes and practical ideas for how to gain strength from life's adversities.

Braden, Gregg. *Walking Between the Worlds: The Science of Compassion*. Radio Bookstore Press, 1997.

> A unique mix of scientific knowledge and spiritual depth, a synthesis of Western thinking and Eastern philosophy. The overall premise is that we are on the brink of major shifts in how the world works and that the usefulness of the old standbys of fear, judgment and polarity are shifting out as part of the overall change.

Cameron, Julia. *The Artist's Way: A Spiritual Path to Higher Creativity*. Jeremy P. Tarcher/Putnam, 1992.

> A delightful invitation to explore the beautiful, mysterious realms of your own creativity. No "talent" required. This book is great for learning to let the creative part of you exist in your everyday life instead of waiting for those "somedays" when you're going to take a painting class or learn to throw a pot.

———. *The Right to Write*. Jeremy P. Tarcher/Putnam, 1998.

> This is an insightful look at writing as a creative process and at writers as people who HAVE to write. There are many forms of writing and not all of them are intended as commercial endeavors—that doesn't change the reality that writers must write.

Dreaver, Jim. The *Ultimate Cure: The Healing Energy Within You*. Llewellyn Publications, 1996.

> The book and the author's life work started because of a health crisis he had to heal from. The book is an account of that healing journey and a blueprint for what anyone needs to do to "discover the happiness that comes from within."

Dossey, Larry. *Reinventing Medicine: Beyond Mind-Body to a New Era of Healing*. Harper San Francisco, 1999.

> Authored by one of the pioneers of mind/body medicine. Offers scientific and medical bases for the effect of the spiritual dimension on physical health.

Dychtwald, Ken. *Age Power: How the 21ˢᵗ Century Will Be Ruled by the New Old*. Jeremy Tarcher/Putnam, 1999.

> A frank discussion of the demographic and economic shifts that are part of the aging of the baby boom. Based on 25 years of research, Dychtwald looks at the largest generation in history and discusses the ramifications of their living "well beyond their eighties and nineties as the 'new old', influencing all of our daily lives." Not a pretty picture since it's based on current assumptions about how all those people are going to spend their time and the country's resources.

Dyer, Wayne. *The Power of Intention: Learning to Co-create Your World Your Way*. Hay House, Inc., 2004.

> Looks at intention in a different light than "willpower" and lays out how to harness it and use it to get your life to be what you want it to be.

Links personal and Divine purpose in a way that makes them far more compatible than what is typically assumed.

———. *Your Erroneous Zone.* Harper Perennial, 1976

The first of Dyer's many books on how to deal with your own needs effectively. Easy to read and revolutionary for its time, it's still a good place to start if you are just discovering you have a right to feel.

Evans, Patricia. *The Verbally Abusive Relationship.* Adams Media Corporation, 1992, 1996.

Everyone who is contemplating marriage or a serious relationship should be required to read this book. Verbal abuse is rampant in this society and it's highly likely neither the "perpetrator" nor the "victim" realize what's happening at the outset. This book provides clear descriptions of what is verbally abusive. (Silence and not being willing to discuss things are every bit as abusive as yelling and name calling.) It falls short on explaining why this is happening and how to stop it, but this is the book to start with to understand what verbal abuse is. (Harriet Lerner's *The Dance of Connection* does a more complete job of demonstrating effective ways to deal with such behaviors.)

Gawain, Shakti. *Developing Intuition: Practical Guidance for Daily Life.* New World Library, 2000.

A practical look at intuition and how to use it. Includes exercises for developing it.

Geissel, Theodore (Dr. Seuess). *Oh, the Places You'll Go!* Random House, 1990.

At one point, one of the big brokerage houses was handing this out to their brokers. Really. It doesn't take a thousand words to say something profound—if you are Dr. Seuess. Read it to your grandkids. You'll be surprised what you learn.

Gladwell, Malcolm. *Blink: The Power of Thinking Without Thinking.* Little Brown and Company, 2005.

> Many decisions have to be made in a split second. The likelihood those decisions are well made depends on how well you understand the context and content area before that moment. Outdated assumptions and erroneous information can be disastrous.

Harkness, Helen. *Don't Stop the Career Clock: Rejecting the Myths of Aging for a New Way to Work in the 21st Century.* Davies-Black Publishing, 1999.

> This felt like rain in the Sahara when I read it! She presents a strong case for continuing to work instead of retiring. And she speaks from experience as well as expertise. The exercises are good, but are mostly aimed at traditional work contexts.

Kaigler-Walker, Karen. *Positive Aging: Every Woman's Quest for Wisdom and Beauty.* Conari Press, 1997.

> Despite the wretched title, her take on why women have been focused on fashion and beauty for millennia is invigorating. The book focuses on our society's preoccupation with women's appearance and offers insights that go beyond worrying about what colors are "in." Good for the guys who love them as well as the women who yearn to get past this level of living.

Kelly, Matthew. *The Rhythm of Life: Living Every Day with Passion and Purpose.* Fireside, 1999.

> This is one of those books that had me writing down quotes on little slips of paper every time I picked it up. Kelly has both a great perspective and a fun way of saying things.

Kepner, Charles, H. and Tregoe, Benjamin B. *The Rational Manager: A Systematic Approach to Problem Solving and Decision Making.* Kepner-Tregoe, Inc, 1965.

Right. You don't really need this book. This is about RATIONAL decision-making. I put it in here in case you want to do some sort of "compare and contrast" work. Then again, if you are trying to decide whether to buy a shoe manufacturing company…

Kirshenbaum, Mira. *Too Good to Leave, Too Bad to Stay.* Plume/Penguin Books, 1997.

A useful resource for those in "iffy" relationships. Kirshenbaum, a psychotherapist, considers different relationship situations and shares her clients' success with staying or leaving in each circumstance. (I found this book helpful after I started to grapple with what I uncovered in Patricia Evans' book on verbal abuse.)

Lerner, Harriet. *The Dance of Connection: How to Talk to Someone When You're Mad, Hurt, Scared, Frustrated, Insulted, Betrayed, or Desperate.* Quill/HarperCollins, 1997.

If you only read one book on this list, read this one. Lerner does an outstanding job of shining light into the shadows of ineffective communication. She shows how to communicate successfully in high stress situations where we care too much about the consequences to find the conversation easy.

Leonard, George, & Murphy, Michael. *The Life We Are Given: A Long-Term Program for Realizing the Potential of Body, Mind, Heart, and Soul.* Jeremy P. Tarcher/Putnam, 1995.

Gives step by step help on designing your entire life as a conscious spiritual practice to enhance every aspect, not just your spirituality, within your ordinary environment (no ashrams required). The authors call the approach Integral Transformative Practice and describe it as "the path that never ends." Even if you don't want to do it their way, it's a great pattern from which to build your own version of a practical, comprehensive, spiritual practice.

Lloyd, Carol. *Creating a Life Worth Living*, HarperCollins, 1997.

One version of a process for reinventing your life—at any age. Lloyd focuses on getting the creative side of yourself into what you do for a living, but you can use these techniques to shape what you want to do in non-paying contexts as well.

Loehr, Jim, and Schwartz, Tony. *The Power of Full Engagement: Managing Energy, Not Time Is the Key to High Performance and Personal Renewal.* Free Press, 2003.

Though aimed at business people and those struggling to de-stress their lives in the corporate setting, the authors' premise is important and worth considering for everyone. The idea is that if you manage your energy well, your time will take care of itself—useful no matter what context you live in.

McKay, Matthew, Rogers, Peter, and McKay, Judith. *When Anger Hurts.* New Harbinger Publications, 1989.

If you are the kind of person who blows up at others, you need to read this book. I was stunned to learn the extent of the damage possible from even one angry outburst. This is a book I lend a lot (and currently my copy is missing—again).

Myss, Caroline. *Anatomy of the Spirit: The Seven Stages of Power and Healing.* Three Rivers Press, 1997.

Myss does an incredible job of weaving the core beliefs of diverse religions into a cohesive explanation of what a soul is all about. It is also a very clear explanation of energy medicine. (This is one I reread—and I don't like to do *anything* twice.)

———. *Why People Don't Heal and How They Can.* Harmony Books, 1997.

Myss looks at the ties between what happens to a body and what the soul that's in it has been dealing or not dealing with. It also presents a vivid and convincing set of arguments for the disastrous effects of practicing "victimology." Her premise is that to get beyond whatever health problems you have, you must deal with the soul issues that are connected to them.

———. *Sacred Contracts: Awakening Your Divine Potential.* Harmony Books, 2001.

This book picks up on the ideas of Myss's earlier ones but builds in the direction of using archetypes to understand your life and move to a higher spiritual plane. (Each of her books stands alone in what it suggests and explains, but each is also part of her growing sense of how to live a spiritually satisfying life.) I was dumbfounded at how much I learned about myself by looking at my life in terms of archetypes.

Northrup, Christiane. *The Wisdom of Menopause: Creating Physical and Emotional Health and Healing During the Change.* Bantam Books, 2001.

A virtual encyclopedia for women and the men who love them. What to expect and what to do about the many effects/changes of menopause. An indispensable resource book written like an informative chat over coffee with a dear, knowledgeable friend, Northrup covers the emotional as well as the physical aspects of the most obvious part of the transition from mother to wise woman.

Schwartz, Tony. *What Really Matters: Searching for Wisdom in America.* Bantam Books, 1995.

America and Americans are seeking and finding Truth in a variety of alternative spiritual disciplines. This book looks at what non-traditional teachers are saying and doing and evaluates each approach. The result is both readable and worthwhile as a starting point for exploring your own spiritual options.

Sedlar, Jeri, and Miners, Rick. ***Don't Retire, REWIRE! 5 Steps to Fulfilling Work That Fuels Your Passion, Suits Your Personality or Fills Your Pocket***. Alpha/Penguin, 2003.

> One of several recent books on how to do more than "nothing" in retirement. Their approach is based on defining the "drivers" in your life and using those to chart a more satisfying course.

Selye, Hans. ***The Stress of Life.*** 1978.

> The book is where "stress" first came into its current usage. The ideas are the result of extensive research the author conducted. Believe it or not, some stress is positive.

Sher, Barbara. ***I Could Do Anything if I Only Knew What It Was.*** Delacorte Press, 1994.

> This is a good book for helping find yourself at any age. Sher takes a systematic approach to dealing with obstacles as well as understanding where your own path would best wind. Besides, she is really fun to read.

———. ***Live the Life You Love: In Ten Step-by-Step Lessons.*** Dell Publishing, 1996.

> An excellent resource for helping yourself figure out what kind of work really lights your fire, although couched in terms of how to do it as your primary source of income. This book is for anyone who's interested in meshing what you love and what you do for a living. Some of Sher's "fact-finding" exercises are unique; for others, she takes familiar exercises several steps farther to give them more power in helping you understand what you really like.

Steinem, Gloria. *Revolution from Within: A Book of Self-Esteem.* Little, Brown and Company, 1992.

> This is not a "feminist book." As she states in her dedication, "This book is intended for everyone—women, men, children, and even nations—whose power has been limited by a lack of self-esteem." I include this book both because the topic is *always* relevant and because it's an awesome example of work that gets done in "the second half."

Stone, Marika and Howard. *Too Young to Retire: 101 Ways to Start the Rest of Your Life.* Plume/Penguin, 2002

> A practical look at a broad variety of ways to move in a new direction when you have the choice to no longer work. It has an extensive list of resources and offers quizzes and exercises to help winnow the kernels of what you really want to do with the rest of your life. (They also have a website that's worth checking out.)

Tharp, Twyla. *The Creative Habit: Learn It and Use It for Life.* Simon & Schuster, 2006.

> This is my most recent "magic book." A friend lent it to me, and I couldn't put it down. Tharp is a world-renown choreographer but what she describes as needed habits for creatives is priceless advice in any context.

Viorst, Judith. *Necessary Losses: The Loves, Illusions, Dependencies, and Impossible Expectations That All of Us Have to Give Up in Order to Grow.* Fawcett Gold Medal, 1985.

> This is another example of what a person can do in the second half of life. It is a monumental work by a best-selling author who went back to school for SIX years to become expert enough in psychology to explore and explain the losses we all must experience in order to grow into our own magnificence.

PERIODICALS

I am hesitant to make a list of these since there seems to be a magazine (or 10) for any kind of interest you can come up with. The two that address this time of life most extensively are: *AARP Bulletin* and *AARP The Magazine,* both published by the American Association of Retired Persons. You don't need to endorse their politics or positions—or even join. (Read it at your local library if you "don't want to be old enough to belong to AARP.") These two periodicals have a wealth of general information in them specifically to help those over 50.

Prevention Magazine, by Rodale Press, does a pretty good job of laying out ways to stay healthy physically and emotionally.

Virtually ANY topic is likely to have an industry trade journal or an enthusiast's publication. These are best discovered by exploring what you're interested in either online or at your local library. Join groups focused on that interest area. Someone will clue you in on which magazines and newsletters are available—and which ones are worth subscribing to, either in hard copy or online.

WEBSITES

The Internet is an absolute boon to information gathering, but be careful. It is also essentially lawless. Anyone can say anything and present it as the truth. There are no official watchdogs you can count on to keep things right. Those wise to cyberspace are also very careful about what they download. My son just removed some objectionable "free" software for me yesterday. I thought it was just for helping me fill out forms. Turns out it's also for tracking every keystroke I make while online. Assess the credibility and validity of the sites you explore and pay attention to what you are doing.

Some of us need a nudge to get on the computer each and every time and some of us need an enforcer to get off to eat or go to bed. I have no intention of trying to suggest how you go about surfing or even telling you to do it. You have to decide. Sometimes that decision is forced by information you have to have NOW. You don't have to wait for the Internet to open in the morning. You don't have to have an appointment to seek the answer to a question. If you want to use it, it can be an awesome tool. But everything I've already said about information on the Internet is still true. There is no one out there making sure that what's up is accurate, current, real, or even honest. So be careful. But have fun, too. The volume of information is amazing.

The following is a smattering of the websites that relate to this stage of our lives—with the exception of www.coolworks.com, which is a clearinghouse for seasonal "jobs in great places" for everyone. Use these—or other sites—as a way to find links or the right key words to enhance your surfing success.

www.aarpmagazine.org

www.aarp.org

www.2young2retire.com

www.coolworks.com

Then, of course, there is ***www.mining-silver.com***.

This is our website and is designed to take you beyond what you found in the book, both by alerting you to new resources and developments and in offering encouragement. The sections are updated regularly. It's also the easiest way to contact us.

CONTACT US

As a culture we HAVE to do a better job of living and using this part of life. Please tell us what you think makes sense for this transition and what you need beyond this book. Mining Silver LLC has been formed to provide resources to help make these years a powerful, happy, balanced time of our lives. Whatever you can tell us about how to help (short of giving you a million dollars) is much appreciated.

Please remember these are also MY best years though. If you don't hear from me right away, I may be on a jetboat on the Snake River or hiking to Machu Picchu.

If you want to write, send snail mail to:

Mining Silver LLC
P.O. Box 65587
University Place, WA 98464-5587

If you want to e-mail us, it's *support@mining-silver.com*.

And if you'd like another copy of this book,
it's easiest to order through our website:
www.mining-silver.com

If you need to reach us by phone, its 253-208-0059.
(Don't be surprised if it goes to Voice Mail.)

INDEX

www.ingramcontent.com/pod-product-compliance
Lightning Source LLC
Chambersburg PA
CBHW031922190326
41519CB00007B/381